973.19
V12m
c.2

Vail, Philip, *pseud.*
　　The magnificent adventures of Henry Hudson.　With
maps by James MacDonald.　New York, Dodd, Mead ₍1965₎

　　217, ₍1₎ p.　maps.　22 cm.
　　Bibliography: p. ₍218₎

8864

DEC
1967 NO 23

　　1. Hudson, Henry, d. 1611.　　ɪ. Title.

E129.H8V3　　　　　　910.0942　　　　　65–17643

Library of Congress　　　　₍5₎

The Magnificent Adventures of

HENRY HUDSON

*Thus much is certain; that he that commands the sea
is at great liberty . . .*

Francis Bacon (1561–1626)

The Magnificent Adventures
of Henry Hudson

 by Philip Vail

WITH MAPS BY JAMES MACDONALD

DODD, MEAD & COMPANY, NEW YORK

For Ruth Ellen Cook

Library of Congress Catalog Card Number: 65-17643
Printed in the United States of America
by The Cornwall Press, Inc., Cornwall, N. Y.

Contents

I. The Furious Overfall   1

II. Arctic Whales and Russian Gold   14

III. The Roof of the World   38

IV. The Jolly Burghers   55

V. The Half Moon   79

VI. Discovery   98

VII. The Great River—and Beyond   113

VIII. The English Tempest   131

IX. Secrets of the Furious Overfall   152

X. The Terrible Winter   173

XI. Mutiny   186

XII. The Fruits of Villainy   197

XIII. Glory and Retribution   212

Principal Bibliography   218

MAPS

Henry Hudson's First Voyage to Spitsbergen   vi

Hudson's Second Voyage to Novaya Zemlya   41

Henry Hudson's Third Voyage, along the East Coast of North America   93

Hudson's Fourth and Last Voyage   159

3085

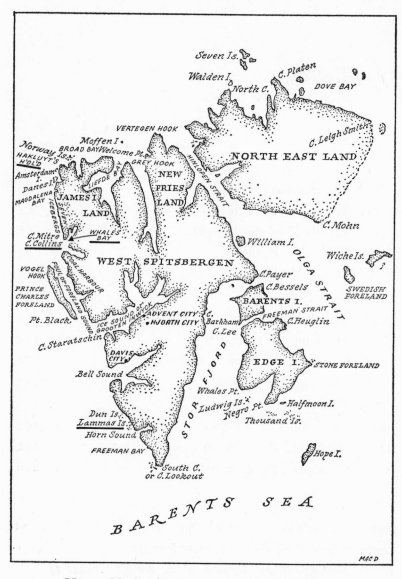

Henry Hudson's first voyage to Spitsbergen.
Names underlined are those used by Hudson.

I

The Furious Overfall

ट**≫**

A SHRIEKING, FREEZING GALE howled down from the unknown
Arctic wastelands across the Atlantic Ocean.

The tiny bark, a frail vessel of no more than forty tons,
was competely at the mercy of the elements. The wind tore
at the sails on her two square-rigged masts, but the canvas
held firm. Then the fabric gave way on her smallest mast,
which was fore-and-aft rigged. The sailors, fifteen in all,
heard the dreaded sound above the howling of the gale, and
some began to pray.

Mammoth gray-green waves, each larger and more menacing than the last, towered above the little ship. Some crashed
down on her, leaving a dirty foam in their wake as they swept
on. Others rocked the bark, and she wallowed helplessly.
She tossed from port to starboard, starboard to port. She
pitched and heaved, her hull of seasoned English oak groan-

ing. Her torment seemed endless, and with each passing, agonizing moment the storm grew worse.

But the master of the bark remained confident of his ability to ride out the gale. And the terrified seamen put their faith in him—and in the Almighty. John Davys was no ordinary captain, and his men well knew it. This voyage, undertaken in the summer of 1587, was his third expedition of discovery and adventure. He knew more of the hitherto unexplored reaches of the northwestern Atlantic Ocean than any man alive. He had discovered scores of islands and channels. He had visited the subcontinent of Greenland, which he knew by the name of Engronland. He had made friends of strange, barbaric people, later to be called Eskimos. He had steered his craft safely between huge mountains of floating ice.

The crew believed him invincible. If any human could find the northwest sea passage to the Orient, Davys was the man. Sailors of every seagoing nation—England and France, Spain and Portugal and Holland—believed that such a passage existed. Davys intended to find it. England would shout his praises; Queen Elizabeth would dub him a knight. Her Majesty's great State Secretary, Sir Francis Walsingham, had promised him as much, in so many words. And small wonder.

England would win the race for the trade of the East. The gold and silk of Cathay would be hers. The silver and rare spices of India would fill the holds of her merchantmen. She would become the wealthiest, most powerful nation on earth. And John Davys would become one of her most honored citizens.

At the moment, however, he had no thought for anything but the raging storm they faced.

Suddenly the wind shifted, blowing now from due west. That change abruptly ended Davys' dream. His foremast snapped, and a jagged piece of heavy wood struck him on the head. He was knocked unconscious.

Fear paralyzed the crew. But Davys' mate was equal to the emergency. Struggling to the quarterdeck, he ordered the captain taken below. Then he sent three men forward to haul in the dangerous, flapping sails from the broken mast. Meanwhile he lashed himself to the wheel.

Some of the men became hysterical when Henry Hudson headed the bark straight into the wind. They believed him mad, and felt certain all of them were doomed.

But the quiet, studious young mate soon demonstrated that he, like Captain Davys, knew the sea. The wheel shuddered and pulled, but Hudson proved far stronger than the crew had believed possible. The bark continued to ride westward into the fierce gale.

For hour after hour Hudson remained at his post. His hands became numb, and more than once he was afraid they had frozen to the wheel. His arms felt as though they were being torn from their sockets. His legs were as heavy as the lead in the spar the bo's'n used to enforce order in the fo'c'sle. But he stayed at his post through the whole, grueling night. He knew he had no choice; if he collapsed, the venture surely would end in disaster.

At last morning came, and the gale subsided. A sailor made his way to the quarterdeck to report that Captain Davys had regained consciousness and was feeling much better. The man blinked in astonishment at Henry Hudson. The mate had relinquished the wheel to the helmsman, but remained on the quarterdeck. He was pacing up and down briskly, and his step was spry, almost lively. No fatigue showed in his face. And he was the only man on the ship who did not appear to need a shave.

That was because of his fair hair, of course. Davys had sometimes teased him, telling him he was so blond he looked like a Norseman. Or a Dutchman. But Hudson cared little about his appearance: he was in command now, albeit temporarily, and there was too much to be done. First he sent his compliments to the captain. Then he ordered breakfast brought to him, and ate with his usual relish. The men could not understand why he remained so slender, for no one's appetite matched his. He calmly consumed two loaves of hard-bread, several dried herring and a bowl of pickled beef; with his meal he drank two tankards of ale. Then, still hungry, he ate a steak of a fish called "holy butt" or halibut, caught only two days earlier.

Now he could devote his entire attention to the tasks at hand. He sent six of the men forward to repair the broken mast. They were tired after the exhausting night and complained. Captain Davys, they said, would let them wait another day. Hudson would not listen.

He raised his voice, lost his temper, and began to curse the bone-weary men. They stood unmoving, silently defying him. So he drew a pistol from his belt, cocked it and threatened to shoot. Then, but only then, they obeyed him.

From that moment the sailors hated the mate. But Henry Hudson did not care. What mattered to him was that the mast and lines were repaired and new sails were hoisted. A sound ship meant everything, the opinions of others nothing. And he had always believed, as he said many years later, that a ship's officer who bowed to the will of his men was a contemptible weakling.

Nevertheless, it would have been strange if he had not reflected on the difference between his attitude and the captain's. Davys was a disciplinarian, of course, as was every master who knew his business, for even the best seamen were rough, unprincipled illiterates who would unhesitatingly cut a man's throat for profit if they believed they could escape undetected.

Yet, even though Davys was firm, his men loved him. He gave orders quietly, and they obeyed his first word. He had the knack of relaxing in their company without losing stature; often he joked with them, and occasionally even ate a meal with them, contrary to custom. Hudson, however, was incapable of dealing with the men so informally. A shy, unassuming and surprisingly gentle man, he felt the need to hold himself aloof at all times. He seemed unable to understand the ways of men who came from a lower social class, and they resented him. So he drove them. Later in his life he would learn the art of cajolery. But never—to the day of his tragic disappearance at the climax of a mutiny—would he become the inspired leader of others.

No matter what his thoughts on the day after the gale, the most exciting event in his life undoubtedly swept everything else from his mind that afternoon. He was taking his ease on the quarterdeck when suddenly he saw an almost unbelievable phenomenon off the port bow.

Davys had discovered it the previous year, 1586, on his second voyage. He had called it the "Furious Overfall."

No one who had ever encountered it could quite believe it. The few men of intellect who had been made privy to Davys' secret had scoffed openly, and Hudson had agreed that nothing so strange could possibly exist. Yet here it was, mysterious, powerful, and frightening.

In fact, Davys' description of the Furious Overfall in his journal had been remarkably accurate. He had written, "We fell into a mighty race, where an island of ice was carried by the force of the current as fast as our bark could sail. We saw the sea falling down into a gulf with a mighty overfall, and moving with diverse circular motions like whirpools, in such sort as forcible streams pass through the arches of bridges."

Before Hudson could move or shout a command, the little ship was swept up in the fast-moving current and carried rapidly westward. *The wind was blowing from west to east, yet the ship was moving westward, against the wind.*

Two of the sailors, who had accompanied Davys the previous year, remained relatively calm. The others immediately lost their heads. Some were certain that sea dragons were taking them to their death. Others, in their terror, invented equally outrageous explanations.

Davys himself came to the quarterdeck, his head bandaged. He stood for a few moments in silence, watching the rushing water. Then, with great regret, he ordered the bark removed from the strange current. The summer was too far advanced for new adventure, he said, and it was imperative that the ship return to England before winter weather made sailing too hazardous.

Henry Hudson's disappointment was overwhelming. The Furious Overfall appealed to his insatiable lust for adventure. As a scientist he was eager to analyze the phenomenon and learn its causes. As an explorer he was desperately anxious to learn where the swift current led. As a sailor, proud of his calling, he wanted to discover all there was to know about this freak of the sea.

But he was helpless. Davys was his superior, and it was his duty to obey the captain.

However, he promised he would return. Charting the current's position with the crude aids to navigation that were the only tools available, he made extensive, detailed maps for his own use. In the cramped privacy of his tiny cabin he wrote detailed notes of all he had seen. He was unwilling to trust any man's memory, including his own, and committed all his thoughts, all his observations, to paper.

The maps and notes were his most treasured possessions. In the years that followed, he studied them often. Gradually the Furious Overfall became an obsession. Through the years he became convinced it was a clue to natural wonders unknown to civilized man, a key that would unlock a door of great discovery.

Two decades were destined to pass before Hudson would be in a position to pursue his own investigation. But when that time came, he would achieve a triumph greater than even he himself imagined possible. Thanks to his daring, skill, and unquenchable curiosity, the boundaries of the known world would be extended. An empire as rich as Cathay, as wealthy as India, would be opened to Western man.

But the mate of the bark, brooding and dreaming in his cabin, could not see that far ahead. In his opinion, the voyage had been a dismal failure. He was sorry he had accompanied Davys on a journey of exploration and discovery. He could have earned far more money as the master of a merchantman in the European or Indian trade. Katherine, his wife, had warned him he was being foolhardy. And events were proving her right.

As the father of two young sons, with a third child on the way, he certainly needed money. Katherine and the boys needed a roof over their heads, and houses in London were expensive. So were food, clothing, all the essentials of life. "We can't live on glory," the practical Katherine had said.

"Glory will lead to gold," Henry had replied. "Remember what happened to the Cabots. Henry the Seventh himself signed Cabot the Elder's commission. And Cabot the Younger sailed under the personal pennant of Henry the Eighth. We English are a seafaring people. We know that in strange seas there are lands no civilized being has ever seen. The men who find them will win wealth as well as glory. Elizabeth deals generously with those who honor her—and England."

Now his brave words mocked him. And his frustration was transformed into deep disgust when Davys dropped anchor in a sheltered Engronland cove. It was true the crew needed fresh water supplies. But the captain went too far when he sought the friendship of the natives.

No Englishman had ever seen people like this strange breed of Eskimos. Short and stocky, with high cheekbones and copper-colored skins, they were primitive barbarians who lived in ramshackle driftwood huts. They dressed in animal skins from head to toe, making it difficult to distinguish men from women. They used whale fat for food and fuel, and even coated their skins with it, which caused them to smell to the high heavens. The fastidious Hudson held himself apart and refused to consort with these savages.

The cheerful Davys remained uninhibited, as usual. Two of the crewmen played lutes, and the captain not only persuaded the sailors to bring them ashore, but himself entertained the Eskimos by singing some of his favorite songs from his native Devonshire. The barbarians were delighted, and reciprocated by presenting Davys with some little figurines carved out of thick fish-bone. Then the Eskimos and Englishmen competed in foot races, running and shouting "like children together," as the captain noted in his journal. Finally everyone sat down together to a feast of boiled walrus meat.

The food was as repugnant to Henry Hudson as the atmosphere, and he ate in stony silence, taking no part in the festivities. He was the only member of the company who felt relief when the bark finally put to sea again.

In spite of his disapproval of Davys' frivolity, he learned much from the captain. He was impressed by a double quadrant Davys had invented, an instrument that enabled an officer to determine a ship's position by the stars with greater accuracy than had ever been achieved previously. He spent long hours on the quarterdeck working with the quadrant, and regardless of his personal opinion of the captain, he appreciated the instrument's worth.

He discovered Davys' greatest secret, too: the master's voyage was self-supporting! Two days were spent searching for cod, and when a school was found, the whole crew went to work hauling huge fish onto the deck of the bark in coarse nets. Cod meat was salted to preserve it, and would bring a high price in the London market. Davys would pay the entire cost of the expedition, pocket a handsome profit from the sale and keep the funds supplied by the noble sponsors of his voyage as well.

The day would come when Hudson would be grateful to his instructor.

But he must have been disgruntled when the bark reached London. Davys received most of the praise, of course, which was customary. But there was precious little glory for anyone. Rumors were being heard everywhere that Philip II of Spain was assembling the mightiest invasion fleet in history. And England was too busy preparing for war to applaud another band of explorers.

In the years that followed, John Davys' fame became greater. He took a major part in the defense against the Spanish Armada in 1588, commanding one of England's largest warships. Thereafter he made another, unsuccessful attempt to find the northwest sea passage to the Orient through the waters "upon the back parts of America." He discovered the Falkland Islands in the South Atlantic, published two books on navigation which were of incalculable help to the mariners who came after him, and then returned to the field of exploration. He was the master of Sir Walter Raleigh's flagship on the great admiral's voyage to Cadiz and the Azores. After the turn of the seventeenth century he made three voyages to the East Indies, and on the last of them, in 1604, was killed by pirates off the coast of Sumatra.

Literally nothing is known of Henry Hudson during that period. He vanished into the anonymity from which he emerged so briefly in 1587. There is no record of his birthplace or date. According to legend, he was a Londoner, the son of a ship's master who had sailed with the Cabots as a mate, but the allegation may be nothing more than a romantic story.

No one has ever learned anything about his early years or education. When did he first go to sea? History has never supplied the answer. What was the maiden name of Katherine, his wife? No one knows. What experience did he acquire prior to the voyage with Davys? The records are silent.

Beyond all else, what were his accomplishments and activities during the two decades between 1587 and his sudden leap into dazzling prominence in 1607? Historians and biographers have searched diligently for centuries, hunting down every clue, but not one scrap of information can be found.

In fact, no one is certain that he actually went with Davys in 1587. Members of the Hudson family itself hold divided opinions on the subject. Some insist that he was Davys' mate in that year. Others claim that the documents purporting to prove that he made this voyage were forgeries, written in

1612 after the news of his shocking disappearance and probable death reached England. There was such great curiosity about him at the time that *Henry Hudson's Journal for 1587* may have been written to satisfy the demand for information about him. Several contemporaries accused one of his sons, Oliver, of being the culprit.

No portrait of Hudson was ever painted. It is believed, but cannot be proved, that he was tall, slender, and blond. Brief references to him in the official and unofficial correspondence of Dutch authorities during the period he was in their employ provide a few, skimpy details.

According to one, "He is as fair as any citizen of Leyden or Amsterdam."

Another said, "His appetite is prodigious, but he is so thin that his bones near burst through his skin."

That he was shy and aloof is proved repeatedly during the five years he held the center of the world stage. His feats demonstrate that he was courageous, sometimes recklessly daring. The journal he kept during parts of his four renowned voyages fills in other details of his character.

Above all, he was an intellectual. Exploration was his passion, and discovery meant more to him than food or drink. He knew every theory concerning the unknown world of his day, and was on intimate terms, as an equal, with the great scientific authorities of his age. Other explorers, Captain John Smith among them, were his friends and held him in great respect.

His fame meant little or nothing to him. He refused to curry favor with his own monarch, King James I, and asked no help from the powerful and wealthy nobles who financed voyages of discovery. He avoided crowds, and popular adulation made him uncomfortable.

He was moody, and spent much of his time alone, when he could. His speech was terse, and he hated verbosity. His temper was razor-edged, and his subordinates lived in fear of him. But he did no man deliberate harm, and his cruelties were partly the result of thoughtlessness, partly the product of an age that was itself cruel and harsh. He was fond of his family, but the Furious Overfall had a stronger lure.

His greatest weakness, which eventually proved fatal, was his inability to lead men.

Conjecture, based on educated guesswork, can fill in some of the gaps in Henry Hudson's life. As he was a mature man with three grown sons when he appeared on the world stage in 1607, it is self-evident that he had spent most of his life at sea. The awe in which he was held by his various employers during this period and the respect accorded him by the governments of England and Holland indicate that he was no ordinary merchant marine master.

Scores, perhaps hundreds, of English and Dutch captains were men of no particular stature. But Hudson was regarded as a personage of consequence by government officials and high-ranking churchmen, noted scholars and famous fellow explorers. So it would appear that, by 1607, he had already made one or more significant voyages of discovery and had established his reputation. It is useless to speculate on other aspects of his past; he may or may not have been a merchant mariner or, perhaps, one of the pirates who preyed on Spanish and other shipping with the semiofficial approval of Elizabeth and her successor, James.

Certainly it is safe to assume that, unless prevented by serious illness, Hudson sailed with the defending fleet that put the Spanish Armada to flight in 1588. Every Englishman even remotely familiar with the sea took part in that effort, and it is inconceivable that a man already a naval officer would not have fought for his country. Hudson's rapport with King James' admirals tends to substantiate the belief that they had been comrades in arms.

Whatever his background may have been, Hudson lived with his family in a fine brick house near the Tower of London in 1607. The building was narrow, but stood three stories high. A vegetable garden in the rear, near the kitchen outbuilding, was tended by Mrs. Hudson and a maidservant. That the family could afford to hire a servant was a sign that the captain was prosperous. So was the location of his home, in a district where well-to-do merchants and other members of the growing middle class resided.

Evidently Henry Hudson himself knew, in 1607, that he was flirting with immortality. In a letter written early in that year to the Reverend Richard Hakluyt, the great geographer of the age and patron of all English explorers, he said, "I take leave of England in a few months to test the theory that a route to Cathay can be found across the half-frozen seas that cover the roof of the world. I shall come to you at Bristol, and with your permission shall study your charts of that region.

"The hopes of my employers are higher than mine that this venture will succeed. I fear the ice may prove too thick. But we shall persevere.

"If the route be not found to the north, I know another. Would there were at [my] disposal all that others have gleaned about my Furious Overfall in the western sea. There, I know, lies the sure sea path to the Indies, and he who finds it will be remembered for all time, even as Drake will not be forgot. I pray with all my heart. Be it by nothern path or western, I would that my name be carved on the tablets of the sea."

II

Arctic Whales and Russian Gold

ह्ब

EVERY AGE HAS ITS HEROES, and none in sixteenth- and seventeenth-century Europe were more dazzling in the eyes of their contemporaries than the adventure-seeking, exploring rovers of the sea. The excitement generated by their discoveries is equaled only in our own time by man's probes into space.

Spurred by such patrons as Ferdinand of Aragon and Prince Henry of Portugal, the pioneer captains found new, uncharted seas, new, unmapped continents. Columbus and Magellan, Balboa and Amerigo Vespucci, changed all of civilized man's concepts of the shape and nature of the earth on which human beings lived.

Nation after nation joined in the frantic race for new territories and the wealth that came from trade with far-distant lands. Sea power became all-important, but monarchs soon learned that power was useless without knowledge. Prince Henry taught all Europe a badly needed lesson when he established his Academy at Lisbon and staffed it with brilliant scientists from the great universities of the West.

By the beginning of the seventeenth century, two geographers stood above the rest. Oddly, both were clergymen. In England there was Richard Hakluyt, Archdeacon of Westminster, who published a never-ending flow of treatises, maps, and charts. In Holland there was the equally brilliant, equally devoted Reverend Peter Plancius, who was considered such a valuable national asset that the government would not permit him to leave Dutch soil.

The great geographers could not work alone, in a vacuum. The raw material they refined and analyzed, sifted and developed, came to them from a remarkable company of practical scientists, the sea rovers. These captains were fearless, insatiably curious, and strangely indifferent to the violent, nationalistic spirit of their times. They explored for the sake of exploring and the joy of adventure. Like the geographers who were the despair of secrecy-loving kings, they were eager to share their discoveries with colleagues from other lands. Many, like Columbus, sailed under flags other than their own.

England was one of the first nations to join the race, thanks to the sagacity of Henry VII. The King hired John Cabot, a native of Genoa and citizen of Venice, to fly the British ensign. He made his first voyage only four years after Columbus' epic journey to the West Indies in 1492. He, and his son Sebastian after him, explored many parts of the North American coast by the middle of the sixteenth century. To them, too, goes the honor of being the first to believe there was a northwest sea passage to the East.

In the decades that followed, England became a great sea power under Henry VIII and Elizabeth I. Native-born sea rovers picked up the challenge of the Cabots. Drake and Hawkins and Raleigh, Frobisher and Davys, charted the Atlantic and the Arctic.

Now, at the start of the seventeenth century, the race had become still more frantic. New rover-adventurers were carrying the English flag for King James. Some, heroes in their own time, are now half-forgotten: Thomas Cavendish and Molineaux, Sir Thomas Smith and George Waymouth. Others have survived through the centuries. There was the opportunistic rogue-of-rogues, Captain John Smith, who founded the first permanent English settlement in North America at Jamestown, Virginia, in 1607, and later gave Cape Cod its name. There was precise, hard-bitten William Baffin, who was impervious to both cold and heat.

Above them all in stature is the enigmatic Henry Hudson.

His thirst for knowledge and yearning for adventure won him a permanent place in the first rank of the world's great explorers. On shore he lived a sedate, almost prim life. At sea he was untiring, ruthless, and cold. He gave his name to a great river and one of the world's largest inland seas. A company bearing his name, still prospering after three hundred years, became a virtual empire in its own right. And his death, like his early life, is shrouded in mystery.

In 1607, when Hudson first became known to the world, England was engaged in a furious three-way race for the domination of northern European trade. Holland took the lead, thanks in part to the genius of Peter Plancius, in part to the discoveries of sea rover William Barents. Lagging a poor third was Imperial Russia. All three nations more or less simultaneously conceived the idea of finding a north*east* passage to the Orient.

Dutch ships piloted by Barents and Oliver Brunel were the

first to sail into the cold waters of the Arctic north of what is now known as the Scandinavian Peninsula. England became increasingly disturbed. The most upset were the factors, or directors, of the Muscovy Company. They were the principal beneficiaries of the northern trade. They stood to gain the most if one of their captains found the northeast route to Cathay. And they would lose the most if they lost the race.

Business was too poor for the company to take chances. The factors tried to interest King James in their projected plan to seek the northeast route. But the vain and surly monarch was busy with too many plans of his own. He graciously gave the Muscovy Company his blessings, but no cash. The factors were forced to finance an expedition themselves.

Their first and most important task was to find a leader, and they hoped he would not charge too much. Their first choice was John Smith, but they learned he had already been hired to take a company of settlers to Virginia.

It was then, in January, 1607, that the name of Henry Hudson first appears in print. At a meeting of Muscovy Company factors in London's Inner Temple, he was suggested as the commander of the expedition. "He is an experienced sea-pilot," the minutes of the meeting said, "and he has in his possession secret information that will enable him to find the north-east passage."

A deputation of factors went to Hakluyt at his Bristol laboratory for advice. The Archdeacon assured them there was no captain better qualified for the post than Henry Hudson.

Was it true, the factors asked, that he was acquainted with a new and secret route to Cathay?

Legend says that Hakluyt merely smiled.

Hudson was hired at once, and he, too, made an immediate

pilgrimage to Bristol. There, in Hakluyt's chart-lined library, the explorer and the geographer spoke freely. The "secret route" was one that both knew well. In fact, anyone who wanted to bother could learn all the details from an eight-year-old pamphlet that had been published, appropriately enough, in Bristol. Both Hudson and Hakluyt knew it as *Thorne's Plan.*

Robert Thorne had been the agent of a prosperous Bristol trading company. His father had been a member of John Cabot's original crew, and the son had developed a strong interest in exploration and navigation. He had written a fervent letter to King Henry VIII suggesting a new route to Cathay. The King had shown little interest in the scheme. Thorne had been piqued, and had published the letter as a pamphlet at his own expense.

Hudson owned a copy. Hakluyt had several. In all probability they pored over it together. Certainly Thorne's opening words offered a ringing challenge to England's master geographer and the seaman who would shortly become his nation's greatest explorer:

"There is no land uninhabitable and no sea unnavigable!"

Hudson and Hakluyt agreed.

They were somewhat less certain of the arguments Thorne had advanced. His idea, in brief, was to sail straight across the North Pole.

No man had ever sailed in those waters, and Hakluyt thought it might be possible that a land mass might impede sea travel.

Hudson believed there was only one way to find out. He would try to sail across the Pole. If unimpeded by land, he would be able to reach Cathay.

Thorne had anticipated the objections of men who would

follow him by almost a century, saying in the pamphlet, "So that if I had faculty to my will, it should be the first thing that I would understand, even to attempt if our Sea northward be navigable to the Pole or no.

"Now then, if from Newfoundlands the sea be navigable, there is no doubt, but sailing Northward and passing the Pole, descending to the Equinoctial line, we shall arrive at the Islands of Cathay, and it should be a much shorter way than any other.

"For the sailors being past this little way which they named so dangerous (which may be two or three leagues before they come to the Pole, and as much more after they pass the Pole) it is clear, that from thence forth the seas and lands are as temperate as in these parts. Then it may be at the will of the mariners, and at their pleasure, whether they will sail by the coasts that be cold, temperate or hot. For thus being past the Pole, it is plain, they may decline to what part they list."

Most of the discussion between Hudson and Hakluyt was devoted to this remarkable theory, which no man had ever put to a test. Thorne had not developed the notion that the climate at the North Pole was mild. This idea had existed for twenty years or more before he had written his document. The basis of the belief was that the Pole was an almost miraculous pinnacle at the apex of the earth. It was a "place of great dignity."

Peter Plancius believed implicitly in this theory, and Hakluyt produced a letter he had received from his distinguished Dutch colleague. "Near the Pole," Plancius wrote, "the sun shines for five months continually; and although his rays are weak, yet on account of the long time they continue, they have sufficient strength to warm the ground (the Pole itself being an island surrounded by sea), to render it temperate, to accomodate it for the habitation of men, and to produce grass for the norishment of animals."

He substantiated his view with a reasonable example. If a small fire is kept constantly lighted in a room, he said, the warmth of the room will be maintained more easily than by means of a large fire which is allowed to die from time to time.

Hakluyt also showed Hudson a communication from another clergyman-geographer, the Reverend Samuel Purchas, who might be termed an imaginative scientist. "If either by North-east or North-west or North a passage be open," he declared enthusiastically, "the sight of the globe (the image of the site of the world) easily sheweth with how much ease, in how little time and expense the same might be effected, the large lines or Merideans under the line, containing six hundred miles, contracting themselves proportionably as they grow nearer the Pole, where the vast line at Circumference itself becomes (as the whole Earth to Heaven, and all earthly things to heavenly) no line any more, but a Point, but Nothing, but Vanity."

The extent to which Hudson took this semipoetic, semitheological effluence seriously is unknown. However, he did write a brief note to the factors saying that his paper work for his departure across the "Point" to the Sea of Chin and the fabulous city of Zipangu was now completed.

When he returned to London, his wife prevailed on him to reconsider the project. Katherine Hudson had been brooding about Zipangu, where the streets were paved with precious stones and the palace of the ruler of Chin was covered with sheets of pure gold. The sum of one hundred pounds, which her husband had accepted as his fee, was too small. He was risking his life, and that of her second son, for a pittance.

Her arguments were valid. The fee was equivalent to approximately three thousand dollars today.

The embarrassed Hudson requested, and was granted, a new meeting with the directors. Although he had accepted their terms, he had not yet signed his contract. So they were forced to give him more money or find another qualified captain. After much haggling, the fee was increased by thirty pounds and five shillings. The reason for the odd sum of five shillings has never been explained to anyone's satisfaction; according to several later seventeenth-century sources, it was intended to pay for the captain's personal stock of ale and wine.

Now Hudson settled down to practical work in earnest. He soon found the ship he considered ideal for his purposes. She was the *Hopewell*, a three-year-old vessel of eighty tons. Fortunately she was already the property of the Muscovy Company, so the factors were not required to spend more of their hard-earned silver for her. She had made six major voyages, two through the Baltic and four down the Atlantic coast to Portugal, so she was known to be seaworthy. Like all commercial ships of the period, she was a bark, with two principal masts and a smaller foremast.

She was made of seasoned oak, but Hudson took the precaution of ordering her seams sealed with fresh gum. There was ample storage room in her hold for provisions, and the captain personally supervised the purchase and storage of food and other supplies. Pickled beef, dried beef, and pickled pork were the main staples. To them were added bags of dried peas, together with carrots, onions, and barley meal. No fish was stored aboard, but several casks of salt were included in the cargo. Hudson intended to cure fish that the crew caught on the voyage. Remembering the lesson he had learned from

Davys, he hoped to bring home enough fish to earn himself an additional profit.

The selection of his crew took surprisingly little time. There were scores of veteran seamen in England, many unemployed. It was a simple matter to find men of ability and experience. His mate was John Colman, who held a master's rating and therefore was qualified to assume his own command. Ten others made up the crew, including the captain's son, John. This young man, although called an officer, slept with the sailors. Only Hudson and Colman had private cabins. The captain also had his own galley, with a stove set in a large box of sand. It was the custom for a master's meals to be cooked separately; he bought his own food supplies, which were stored in a private larder.

By mid-April, 1607, all was in readiness, and on the nineteenth the entire crew attended a special service at the Church of St. Ethelburga in Bishopsgate. Mrs. Hudson and Mrs. Colman were there with their husbands, and the factors came down the aisle in a body, accompanied by retainers. The departing adventurers took Holy Communion, special prayers were offered for their safe return, and the congregation listened to a sermon entitled, "God's Known Realm."

Spiritually refreshed, Hudson and his men repaired to the *Hopewell*, anticipating an early departure. But foul weather delayed them for almost two weeks. England was wrapped in a thicker-than-usual spring fog, and then a gale descended on the British Isles. The skies did not clear until May 1, and on that date the expedition set sail.

Twenty-six days later they stood off the Shetland Islands, and Hudson ordered soundings taken. The bottom, he reported in his log, was black, sandy, and filled with ooze. The sea floor was covered with yellow shells.

By May 30 he had traveled so far north that the compass, affected by the Magnetic Pole, began to misbehave. "This day I found the needle to incline seventy-nine degrees under the horizon," he complained.

The *Hopewell* sailed north of the Faeroe Islands and Iceland, and on June 13 Engronland was sighted. Hudson, like Davys and Frobisher before him, mistakenly believed that the southern portion was a relatively small island separated from the mainland by a strait or channel. For the next eight days he sailed cautiously northward, keeping the east coast of Greenland in sight. One morning, soon after dawn, the lookout in the crow's nest, James Young, spotted a hitherto unknown spit of land jutting into the sea. Hudson called it Young's Cape, a name which has been retained through the centuries. He also called a nearby high hill Mount of God's Mercy.

The region was one of the most desolate in the Arctic, uninhabited except for an occasional, stray musk-ox. Hudson described it in his log: "We saw some land on head of us, and some ice. It being a thick fog, we steered away northerly. In the morning our sails and shrouds froze. All the afternoon and evening it rained; and the rain froze. This was a very high land, the most part covered with snow. The nether part was uncovered. At the top it looked reddish, and underneath a blackish clay, with much ice lying about it."

The next week was miserable and inconclusive. The current, Hudson noted, moved toward the southwest. The bark drifted toward the east, still inching northward, and eventually moved toward Greenland again. Hudson failed to realize he had made another contact with the huge island subcontinent. Thinking it was a new land, he called it Hold-with-Hope.

The most exciting aspect of his discovery was the seeming

confirmation of the theory that the weather would become warmer as the party drew nearer the North Pole. What Hudson failed to take into consideration, of course, was that temperatures inevitably were higher now, in late June.

"This land," he exulted in his log, "is very temperate to our feeling. It is a main highland, nothing at all covered with snow; and the north part of that main highland was very high mountains, but we could see no snow upon them."

In spite of his pleasure, however, he was deeply troubled. According to everything he had ever learned, there should have been open sea everywhere this far north. The presence of any land whatever disputed the convictions of Hakluyt and Plancius.

He was also afraid he had done something that would cause him to be severely criticized by the Muscovy Company factors, and at this time started keeping a private journal in addition to his official ship's log. By sailing northwest instead of due north, he had deliberately disobeyed orders. He had been assigned the mission of finding the shortest, direct route to the Orient across the Pole.

But the lure westward had been too strong for him. He was curious about Engronland, and frankly confessed in his new journal that he had wanted to learn more about it. Trying to justify himself, he wrote, "It might as well have been open sea as land, and by that means our passage should have been the larger to the Pole. And considering we found land contrary to what our cards [charts] make mention of, we accounted our labor so much the more worth. And for ought that we could see, it is like to be a good land, and worth the seeing."

Hudson had not realized he had strayed so far from the prescribed course. The older of his charts showed Greenland as a bulbous peninsula connected to Norway and jutting to the northwest. The newer showed a few miles of open sea between northern Norway and Greenland. He had not anticipated that he would sail many hundreds of miles off his course.

The sun was above the horizon day and night. Some of the men became irritable, but the younger members of the crew, among them John Hudson, declared they required less sleep than when the nights were dark. The captain himself was fascinated by the phenomenon and unfailingly mentioned it each day in his log.

One afternoon Colman called him to the rail to see a grampus swimming lazily around the ship. The creature was soon joined by two others. The superstitious seamen regarded the trio as omens of evil. Four sailors requested that the party turn back to England at once, but Hudson flatly refused.

Instead he made notes, studying the strange and ferocious sea beasts for hours. A grampus is sometimes described as a large breed of dolphin but is more familiarly known as "the killer whale." Its usual prey is the larger, more docile whale, but it also eats tuna, cod, and other large fish. Hudson somberly recorded in his journal that he had once seen a sailor devoured by a grampus when the unfortunate man had fallen overboard. He gave no details, but obviously could understand why his men were apprehensive.

The largest of the trio, he estimated, was twenty-five feet long, "with a girth like unto a stallion's." The smallest was approximately seventeen feet long. All three had sharp yellowish white teeth. They circled the *Hopewell* continually for twenty-four hours, perhaps because the cook had thrown some refuse overboard.

Eventually their proximity made the whole crew so nervous

that Hudson abandoned his plans to lead an expedition ashore. Instead he tried to sail north, but his progress was slow because of ice packs in the sea.

Finally, at six o'clock on the morning of June 27, the lookout spotted the land that Barents had discovered and named Spitsbergen. Hudson, with English perversity, insisted on calling it Newland. As the days followed, the *Hopewell* moved north through this Arctic archipelago. The many islands appeared barren. Mountains, jagged and snow-covered, rose five thousand feet and higher above sea level. Ice crusts prevented the captain from sailing too close to shore, and desolate rocks made the land even more uninviting. The men saw only a few patches of greenish brown moss.

A storm, the hardest encountered on the voyage, was terrifying. Icy winds blowing down from the north could freeze a man in his tracks if he stood still for as long as five minutes Hudson, pacing up and down his tiny quarterdeck to keep warm, managed to sail into a semiprotected cove. But the effort was almost too great for the entire company. The captain drove the men without mercy, permitting no one to go below until he had dropped his port and starboard anchors. Then only were the men allowed to seek the comparative warmth of their quarters. Hudson himself remained on deck with Colman, intending to heave their "great sea-anchor" over the side as a last precaution. But the weather proved too severe. They struggled for almost two hours, but were unable to inch the anchor over the side. At last they gave up when the lines froze.

For eighteen hours the captain huddled beside his stove. Every half-hour he fought his way up to the quarterdeck to assure himself that the *Hopewell* was not being blown out to sea or swept onto the rocky shore. During that time he neither ate nor slept.

As soon as the storm subsided he tried to take advantage of better weather, but fog closed in. The next day snow fell steadily. Hudson doggedly continued his voyage and tried hard to prepare accurate charts of this unknown realm. He admitted privately, in his journal, that he was completely lost.

Neither then nor in the bewildering days that followed did he realize, even remotely, that he would soon stumble upon treasures as valuable as the cities of gold and gems he was trying to reach.

Suddenly, early in July, the weather improved. The sun was warm, the wind gentle, the sea calm. The men spent a day repairing a minor leak in the hull and mending the rigging. Hudson noted that many seals were climbing onto the rocks. Late that day he saw two strange creatures "which I judged to be sea-horses or morses." No civilized man had yet identified a living walrus.

For almost two weeks he sailed in and out of the channels connecting the islands. Here and there he saw tiny polar willows, none higher than two feet. And on one island was a miniature birch with green leaves. The entire crew lined the maindeck rail to stare at it.

July 14, 1607, was a memorable day for Henry Hudson. Had he achieved nothing of consequence later in his life, he nevertheless would have acquired enduring fame for his discovery on that occasion. Because of it, the factors of Muscovy Company were destined to become wealthy beyond their wildest dreams.

Shortly before noon the *Hopewell* nosed into a huge, placid bay. John Hudson was sent forward with a leaded line and took frequent soundings, which were remarkably accurate. At the entrance the water was thirty fathoms deep. Just inside it was twenty-six fathoms. Then it became too deep to measure. Hudson's equipment did not permit him to take soundings of more than one hundred fathoms. In later centuries scientists found that the greater part of the bay is two hundred and fifty fathoms deep.

Once inside the bay, the men found themselves in an incredible world. The waters were literally teeming with scores, perhaps hundreds, of mammoth whales. These enormous sea mammals were neither disturbed nor frightened by the unexpected appearance of the ship. A few played about, but the majority seemed content to drift. They proved tame beyond belief. One swam under the ship and rubbed against the keel. The *Hopewell* listed alarmingly to starboard, "yet by God's mercy we had no harm," the captain wrote in his log.

Slowly, proceeding with infinite caution, the bark inched toward the inner side of the bay. There, no more than one hundred feet from land, Hudson cast anchor. He tried to count the whales in the bay. The crew joined in but soon tired of the sport, and the captain found the task too much for him. "There are more whales in the bay than ever any man could number," he said that night in his journal.

Colman was anxious to go ashore, as were Bo's'n William Collins and several other members of the crew. They had been cooped up on board the bark for two and a half months, and the lure of the land, combined with the springlike weather, proved irresistible. Hudson granted permission for a party to row ashore in his gig.

Watching them from the quarterdeck, he noted that he could no longer see his breath in the air. This observation confirmed his belief that the theory about a mild Polar climate was true.

But no sooner had the men stepped ashore than a fierce gale blew up, seemingly out of nowhere. Outside the bay the wind raged and the sea became mountainous. Hudson gaped at the tempest beyond the bay's entrance. Inside, the water remained calm, and the high surrounding cliffs held the winds in check.

Then a fog descended which was so dense that Hudson was unable to see his own prow from the quarterdeck. The shore party was trapped on land, and he prayed that no harm would come to the men. After two hours of anxious waiting, the fog lifted as suddenly as it had descended, and Colman brought his party back to the *Hopewell*.

Their report was the most encouraging news of of the entire voyage. "Life can be sustained in this strange and remote place," Hudson wrote confidently in his log. He felt so sure of himself that he repeated the sentence in his journal, carefully underlining each word.

The evidence he presented in an orderly fashion was conclusive:

1. The men brought back the teeth of "many sea-horses."

2. They brought back "a dozen and more deer horns."

3. They had found a stream of clear, running water. All tried it and declared it "the best that ever they had drunk." In fact, their description of it was so enticing that the captain sent a second party ashore to replace the stagnant water in the drinking casks.

4. The men came upon a flock of wild geese, "as plump as any will be seen strutting in the pens of a Middlesex farm."

5. They had also come upon the tracks of two different kinds of animals. Colman positively identified one as the "footings of a fox." He and the bo's'n agreed, after a lengthy dis-

cussion, that the other was probably a bear, "the most savage inhabitant of all the comfortless lands of the north."

6. As a souvenir, the mate brought Hudson a large piece of "whalebone ivory." Hudson estimated its worth at twenty pounds.

7. Another souvenir, picked up as a curiosity, proved to be even more exciting. The captain believed it to be a lump of pure coal, a guess that was confirmed after his return to London.

The meat of fowl and other animals, including, of course, whales, awaited civilized men at Whales Bay, as Hudson named the place. There was ample drinking water and coal to be used as fuel.

It was needless for him to add that every part of the whale was valuable. The meat was edible. The bone was tougher than iron. The carcass, reduced by boiling, produced oil that had a thousand uses. And ambergris, a substance taken from the intestines of the whale, was the base used in making perfume; the ambergris alone was worth far more than the gems of Cathay and the spices of the Indies.

Apparently the idea of claiming a share in the potential wealth did not cross Hudson's mind. Unlike Drake and Raleigh, who acquired fortunes, he cared only about discovery for its own sake. No hint of personal greed appears in either his log or journal. And nothing in his later conduct indicated that he wanted the Muscovy Company to give him a partnership. Such a demand would have been within his rights, but he remained indifferent to money until the day of his death.

Now, late on the evening of July 14, he was anxious to leave Whales Bay. The *Hopewell* weighed anchor as soon as the storm subsided. Summer was passing, and the captain wanted to cross the North Pole as soon as possible.

For the next twenty-four hours he sailed up a part of the Spitsbergen coast he called "The Seven Icebergs." The faces of the glaciers the company saw were a radiant blue-green. Even the sailors, who were not noted for their sense of aesthetic appreciation, were impressed.

But thoughts of lovely colors had to be put aside on July 16. "Everywhere," Hudson wrote gloomily in his log, "there is an abundance of ice compassing us about by the north and joining to the land." It was impossible for him to continue his voyage north.

But he refused to give up. He told the crew they would sail around the southern tip of Spitsbergen and make another try up the eastern coast. The men grumbled, but the captain remained firm. In the next two weeks he made a desperate effort to carry out his mission. But the Artic cold defeated him.

Hopes rose one morning when a member of the crew killed a red-billed bird. The mere fact that the bird was in that icy region "proved" to Hudson that the weather still farther north would be mild.

But that afternoon the company suffered its hour of greatest danger on the entire voyage. A thick fog rolled down from the north, drastically reducing visibility. Hudson proceeded cautiously under less sail. Suddenly he heard a strange noise. It was a low, deep rumble that gradually became louder, more menacing.

He realized that the *Hopewell* was being drawn toward the ominous sound, and tried to change course. But the swell was too strong. The bark crept closer. Now the men could hear nothing but the harsh noise. Its vibration was so intense that the dishes and tankards in the captain's galley trembled. His sword fell from a bulkhead peg in his sleeping cabin. He could do nothing, and the men were terrified.

At last he saw the cause of the disturbance. Directly ahead was an ice pack. The fog lifted, and from the quarterdeck Hudson could make out nothing but ice before him. Here and there it was heaving and grinding as the swells crushed mammoth slabs together.

Hudson had no way of knowing that he had reached the Great Ice Barrier that was to prevent explorers from reaching the North Pole for centuries. But his scientific curiosity was greater than his fear, and he wrote furiously in his log, describing the awesome phenomenon. Probably he would have considered it an empty honor had he realized that for the next two hundred years men would call the barrier by his name.

The plight of the *Hopewell* became worse. The captain had to put away his log. All hands tried in vain to halt the bark's steady drift toward the ice pack. Hudson ordered the boat lowered. Taking command in the gig himself, he made a desperate effort to warp the ship away from the ice. The men used poles, hooks, bare hands. Their puny labors were useless.

Hudson was afraid the frail boat would be smashed between the *Hopewell* and the ice pack. So he ordered the men back to the bark. There was nothing to do now but pray, as it appeared that soon the ship would be a splintered wreck.

Miraculously the sailors' prayers were answered. A strong wind blew up from the northwest. Hudson ordered all sails hoistered. Slowly, painfully, the *Hopewell* crunched off the edge of the barrier into the waters of the Arctic. Then she began to edge away from the ice. A quarter of an hour later she was completely in the clear.

The captain held a southerly course as long as the wind

lasted. He spent thirty-six hours on the quarterdeck without sleep. The men remained at their posts, too. All were over-joyed when the now familiar southern tip of Spitsbergen came into view.

Hudson, like his men, believed that an actual miracle had been responsible for their salvation. "The wind," he wrote in his journal, "was the first from the northwest that has blown in all the days we have sailed in these northern seas. There had been many from all other faces of the earth. But even in tempests, none had blown from that direction. God gave us thankful hearts for so great deliverance."

He cast anchor offshore and held Divine Services in his main cabin. He read from the Book of Psalms, and the men sang a hymn.

Then he made a momentous announcement. It was im-possible to cross the North Pole from the direction of Spits-bergen, he said. Therefore he intended to sail for England. The men cheered so loudly that a pair of gulls resting on a nearby rocky promontory "took fright and flight."

On August 1 the lookout spotted Bear Island, discovered by William Barents a few years earlier, the halfway point between the northern tip of the Scandinavian Peninsula and Spitsbergen. Strong winds from the northeast caused the bark to drift off her course, and a few days later the captain saw another, uncharted island. He placed it carefully on his map, calling it Hudson's Tutches. Ironically, the little island was frequently rediscovered in the next few years. For more than half a century the English used Hudson's name for it, but eventually adopted the name given it by a Dutch explorer, Jan Mayen.

On August 15 the *Hopewell* came to the Faeroes Islands and put into port. Spoiled meat was replaced by fresh, water casks were refilled. "I ate an Italian salat," Hudson noted in his journal. "The taste, after so long without greens, was pleasing to my tongue."

In mid-September the bark finally cast anchor at Tilbury in the Thames River. The *Hopewell* had returned home, and her voyage was at an end.

Henry Hudson's personal estimate was that he had failed. He had been unable to sail across the North Pole, and a short sea route to the Orient was still just a dream.

The factors of the Muscovy Company took a far different view. The captain's report on Whales Bay electrified all England. The factors of the company realized they had acquired a far more lucrative source of income than Russian gold.

Hudson went off to Bristol to confer with Hakluyt, who agreed that a vast portion of the Arctic could no longer be regarded as a navigable approach to the North Pole. He, like all other scientists and explorers, appreciated the enormous contribution Hudson had made to man's knowledge of the far north.

The factors neither knew nor cared. So many nobles and other wealthy men now clamored for shares in the Muscovy Company's ownership that the stock tripled in value before Christmas. The factors diplomatically made King James a free gift of shares worth two thousand pounds. Apparently it did not cross their minds to give Henry Hudson anything except hearty congratulations.

Within weeks of the explorer's return, the merchants began intensive preparations for their attack on the Spitsbergen whales. It took little or no time for them to learn that literally no one in England was familiar with the science of whale killing. The only experts in Europe were Basques, who augmented their living as fishermen by spearing whales in the Bay of Biscay. A representative of the Muscovy Company was sent to southern France to hire instructors.

A fleet of special ships was made ready for departure to the Arctic the following spring. The Basques who came to England informed their new employers that huge vats were needed to reduce whale blubber to soap, so special caldrons were made in a foundry northwest of London. Meanwhile dozens of eager volunteers were signed as whale hunters and workers.

Foreign ambassadors had heard rumors of Hudson's discovery, and word spread rapidly when the Muscovy Company began to hire men for its new commercial venture. The Dutch minister rode out into the country in his carriage, saw the large caldrons being made, and immediately sent off a long letter to his country's Foreign Secretary. The Dutch vigorously recruited their own fleet, and at the same time began the manufacture of copper caldrons, which they considered superior to iron.

Then the Dutch government sent a formal protest to Great Britain, claiming that Spitsbergen was their property by right of prior discovery. The government of King James literally ignored the note. Other nations were alerted by the flurry, and before the winter of 1607–8 came to an end, every power in Europe was planning its own assault on the Arctic whale.

The English were the first to reach Spitsbergen in the spring of 1608. Three Muscovy Company ships sailed into deserted Whales Bay, which was destined to be occupied continually for more than a century. Two weeks later the Dutch came and set up their camp only a few hundred yards from the British. The two groups established amicable relations, as there were enough whales in the bay for all. When the French, Portuguese, and Scandinavians sailed to Spitsbergen, it was found that there were whales in virtually every inlet and cove of the entire archipelago. The boom was on.

Eventually the Dutch established a whole town in north-western Spitsbergen. They called it Smeerenburg, which the English translated as Blubbertown. Carpenters were paid bonuses to sail to the Arctic and build houses. Barbers and tailors went north. Competition for experienced workmen became so intense that cooks and bakers were paid exorbitant wages in the hopes of luring men. The enterprising French even transported a band of young women of dubious virtue to the Arctic, but the girls found the atmosphere somewhat less than congenial, and this experiment was not repeated.

The bakers enjoyed enormous popularity. Each morning, when they took huge loaves of smoking bread from their ovens, horns were blown to herald the tidings. Men of many nationalities hurried from one kitchen to another for the delicacy before beginning their day's work.

The competition became so intense that King James issued an exclusive patent to the Muscovy Company. In it he declared that Spitsbergen belonged to England, and forbade the hunting and killing of whales there by others. He and his government were in no position to enforce the decree except by resorting to full-scale war, however. So the Dutch thumbed their noses at England by publishing a counterdecree of their own. The French, Spaniards, Portuguese, and others did not bother. They were too busy killing whales.

Then "pirate poachers" began to appear. Men operating under no authority other than their own sailed north, caught whales, and vanished again. Murders and other crimes of violence became so common that the various governments were compelled to send special constables to the Arctic to keep the peace.

Whales were not the only creatures slaughtered. Seals were killed in vast numbers, as were walruses. Bear Island and Jan Mayen Island—"Hudson's Tutches"—also became popular hunting grounds for the seal and walrus. Then Russian hunters roamed inland through the mountains of Spitsbergen, and made fortunes on bear pelts. The desolate coasts that Henry Hudson had seen were heavily populated down to the present century, when Spitsbergen was finally awarded to Norway by an international treaty.

It has been estimated that from the time of Hudson's discovery in 1607 to the outbreak of the American War of Independence in 1775, no fewer than 100,000 whales were killed at Spitsbergen. The walrus became virtually extinct, and the reindeer survived only because it had no commercial value.

Oddly, the valuable coal deposits were utilized only for local purposes until the twentieth century. Men boiled whale blubber over coal fires, but no coal was exported. That situation changed drastically when tests proved that the deposits of both soft and hard coal were of excellent quality. Mines have since been operated throughout the islands down to the present day.

By the early months of 1608 Henry Hudson was renowned throughout Europe for his momentous discovery. A year later his fame had doubled, and he could have named his own price to lead whale-hunting expeditions to Spitsbergen. But he was not interested. In spite of his wife's anguished protests, he rejected several lucrative offers.

He had far more important fish to fry than making fortunes for others—or for himself. He was more determined than ever to find a northeast passage to the Orient. Whale killing was a relatively tame, commercial sport, and he could not resist the exciting, demanding call of the unknown.

III

The Roof of the World

გ&

WHILE OTHER MEN planned their attacks on the Spitsbergen whales, Henry Hudson sat alone in his study. There, carefully analyzing the maps he had made, he digested all the knowledge he had acquired on his first voyage. He made several trips to Bristol to confer with Hakluyt. And when the Archdeacon came to London, he dined frequently at Hudson's house.

The explorer also corresponded freely with Plancius in Holland. The two men, indifferent to national rivalries, exchanged information, theories, ideas. Gradually a new scheme took shape in Hudson's mind. The Great Ice Barrier had blocked his approach to the North Pole on his first expedition. But he had reason to believe there might be free, open sea farther to the east.

There was seemingly valid reason for his opinion. Both Hakluyt and Plancius knew that a strange, unexplored land lay somewhere in the northern Arctic, above the coasts of

Russia. There had been hints of its existence for centuries. It was mentioned in vague Norse and Danish legends that had reached England in the eleventh century, during the reign of William the Conqueror. Hakluyt had also accumulated scraps of evidence from occasional travelers to Russia.

The mystery-loving Russians were secretive, and would neither confirm nor deny that they knew of such a land. But, through a stroke of luck, a British merchant who spent several weeks each year in St. Petersburg had become acquainted with two Russian hunters. Both admitted they had made journeys by sea to a large island, bitterly cold, far north of the European mainland. One called the place Novgorod. Hakluyt had tried in vain to learn more from the Russians.

They had been afraid to speak freely to the special emissary he sent to St. Petersburg. Under Russian law, a man who revealed to foreigners information concerning Russia could have his tongue cut out. Or, if the offense was considered serious enough, he might be drawn and quartered. It was useless to question Russians, or to ask the cooperation of the Tsar's government.

But Hakluyt had gathered some data from other sources. Sir Hugh Willoughby, an English explorer, had first reported the existence of a strange country in northern waters. That had been in 1553. He had called the place Gooseland. Three years later another Englishman, Stephen Borough, had actually landed there and confirmed its existence.

He had spent many weeks there, and had carried home a detailed report of his findings. Oddly, they had attracted little attention, and part of his work had been lost. But Hakluyt was in possession of several facts:

Borough had called the place Novaya Zemlya. This distinctly Russian-sounding name seemed to establish beyond all reasonable doubt that the land was indeed known to the Tsars.

Novaya Zemlya consisted of two large islands.

These islands extended from north to south. East of them was a "placid" sea.

Plancius had further data for Hudson. William Barents had visited Novaya Zemlya in 1596. He had actually spent several winter months at an inlet on the northeastern coast. Plancius failed to say whether he had reached it by sailing around the northern tip of the upper island, or whether he had reached it through a channel that divided the islands. In any event, to the east of the islands was a body of water called the Kara Sea. Plancius did not say whether this was a name Barents had given it or whether he had taken a Russian name.

The latter seemed probable to Hudson. He and Hakluyt agreed, too, that the Kara Sea and the "placid" sea mentioned by Borough were probably one and the same.

Hudson was excited by the possible existence of a channel between the two islands. By sailing through it into the Kara Sea and heading northeast, he believed he could reach the Pole. He realized this view was nothing more than an unsubstantiated theory, but he was willing to risk his life in an attempt to prove it.

He approached the factors of the Muscovy Company, telling them no more than he felt necessary. It was enough for them to know he thought he knew of a hitherto unexplored route to Cathay. The factors were so pleased with his discovery of Whales Bay they were happy to give him almost anything he wanted. Only one brief meeting was held, and agreement was quickly reached.

The company would finance a second voyage of exploration. Hudson would be given a free hand in the selection of his crew, and could take as many men as he wanted. The com-

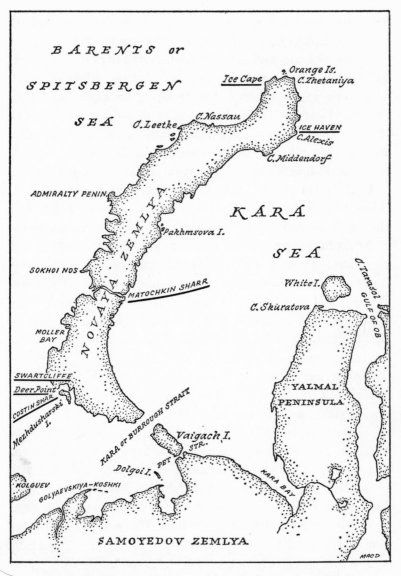

Hudson's second voyage to Novaya Zemlya.
Names underlined are those used by Barents and Hudson.

pany would gladly spend money to strengthen the hull of the *Hopewell* to make her safer in ice-strewn water.

There was one additional improvement Hudson demanded. He believed it imperative to carry a bigger, stronger ship's boat. His exploration of the Spitsbergen coast had been hampered because his gig had been frail, and he felt he could do a far more thorough job with a better boat. It is impossible to determine whether the factors were unimaginative, stupid, or both. Whatever the reason, they balked at this demand.

Hudson threatened to walk out and find other sponsors. The directors were afraid he meant it, and finally voted him the funds to have a boat made according to his specifications.

Again he showed no interest in lining his own pocket, and signed a contract identical with the previous one. Obviously he could have commanded a larger sum, but apparently the thought did not cross his mind. Katherine was sorely disappointed and quarreled with him. But Hudson refused to demand more money for himself. There was so much work to do, and so little time.

He increased his crew by four men. Only his son, John, and two of the seamen were veterans of the Spitsbergen voyage. Colman and most of the original crew had had their fill of discovery, and planned to make their own fortunes in Spitsbergen. Therefore the captain had to recruit new men.

Knowing the Arctic now, he deliberately selected the strongest, toughest seamen he could find. They were a rough lot, but he seemed confident of his ability to handle the men.

As his mate he chose Robert Juet. The reason for this association is a mystery down to the present day. "Juet," Hudson wrote to Archdeacon Hakluyt, "is filled with mean tempers." The mate was fifty years old, which was considered elderly in the seventeenth century. His own journal and letters reveal him as a hard-bitten cynic, a jealous man who hated to take orders from anyone. He disliked Hudson from the outset, and at times his attitude to his superior was barely civil. The best that could be said for him—and Hudson obviously thought it meant a great deal—was that he was a seaman of vast experience.

Larger quantities of meat than on the last voyage were stored in the hold, Hudson having learned that the men kept warmer when they ate beef or pork than when their diet was based on bread, oatmeal, and peas. He also carried enough muskets to arm every man and purchased a small cannon, which he placed under lock and key in a hold reserved for his private use. The men were given access to the muskets from the outset.

On Friday, April 22, 1608, a large crowd gathered at St. Katherine's Wharf in London. An Anglican clergyman said a special prayer for the captain and his crew, who then went on board the *Hopewell*. Juet, who had not taken part in the religious service, was entertaining friends in his quarters, and Hudson was forced to send the guests ashore so he could sail on the afternoon tide. "The nose of Master Juet," he wrote in his journal, "was put much out of joint. When I desired to retire to my sleeping-cabin, J. was still in foul humors, and had to be summoned to take the watch."

The voyage had begun inauspiciously.

Routines of shipboard life were undisturbed for a month. At the end of that time the bark approached the Lofoten Islands, off the west coast of Norway, and there encountered thick fog. The weather suddenly turned very cold, and several members of the crew became sick. Of this number, only Philip Staffe, the carpenter, was confined to his hammock.

The *Hopewell* continued to sail north, taking advantage of favorable winds in spite of the fog. As the ship approached North Cape, the weather cleared and a number of Norwegian fishing boats were sighted. Staffe, who had recovered his health, was ordered to make a mast for the *Hopewell*'s new boat, and Juet grudgingly supervised the cutting and sewing of a sail for it.

Soundings were taken on June 7 with new equipment Hudson was carrying, and bottom was struck at one hundred and fifty fathoms. The following day he could not find the bottom at one hundred and eighty fathoms, and confided in his journal that his hope of finding a deep-water channel to the Orient was strong.

The next morning the captain noted that the sea was a distinctive blackish blue in color. He expressed the opinion, based on his previous experience, that he was approaching ice. Less than twenty-four hours later the lookout spotted ice, the first seen on the voyage. Hudson was the first to record the relationship of the color of the sea to the proximity of large quantities of ice.

At four in the afternoon the ice floes became thicker, but Hudson was determined to remain on a northerly course as long as possible. The going soon became too much for him, however, and when chunks of ice larger than the *Hopewell* began to scrape against the ship's side, he turned toward the southeast. Four hours later the bark was in the clear again, but the sea became rough and remained turbulent for the better part of a week.

June 15 was a memorable occasion. On that day two of the seamen, Robert Raynar and Thomas Hilles, saw a mermaid. Raynar was scrubbing the deck with a soft holystone, a chore sailors always hated, when he caught sight of her.

He shouted, and Hilles joined him. They started at her. "She came close to the ship," Hudson solemnly declared in his log, "looking earnestly on the men." Then a wave flipped her over, and she vanished as abruptly as she had appeared.

The captain, interested as always in scientific phenomena, questioned the pair at length. For posterity's sake he described her in infinite detail: "From the navel upward, her back and breasts were like a woman's, her body as big as one of us. Her skin was very white; and her long hair, hanging down behind, of color black. In her going down [they] saw her tail, which was like the tail of a porpoise, and speckled like a mackerel." Neither Hudson nor any member of his crew doubted the existence of mermaids. They had been reported by too many sailors of too many nationalities to be discredited.

The sail northward was resumed, but on June 18 the bark once again reached the Great Ice Barrier. Hudson skirted its edge, inching toward the southeast only when forced to do so. Gulls infested the area. They were overhead, on the surface of the sea, and perching on chunks of floating ice. It was unusual to find so many birds this far north, and Hudson observed them closely. He finally came to the conclusion that the sea in this area was rich in fish.

The ship passed many small islands, all snow-covered. Juet argued that they were ice floes, not islands.

On June 26 the lookout spotted the high ground of a large island in the distance. Hudson studied his charts and knew he was approaching Novaya Zemlya. But the ice became so thick that he had to abandon all hope of sailing around the northern tip into the Kara Sea.

His only chance lay in finding the alleged passage between the two main islands. No one was certain that such a channel actually existed. No maps could tell him how to proceed.

Juet hinted to the captain, within earshot of several sailors, that it might be wise to return at once to England. The crew became uneasy.

Hudson kept his plans to himself. Maneuvering constantly, he approached the barren shore of Novaya Zemlya, found a sheltered cove, and dropped anchor there. Juet was sent ashore with four of the men to fill the casks with fresh water.

To the mate's astonishment, the land was far from barren, and the sun was unexpectedly hot. Juet had to remove his doublet, and the rays burned his bare arms. Melting snow ran down the slopes of every mountain and every hill. Blades of sturdy, green grass were pushing up through a thin coating of the previous winter's ice. One of the men found a cluster of tiny, white flowers in a sunny, sheltered nook. Juet himself discovered a bed of bright pink flowers. He picked them, and Hudson subsequently noted in his journal that "their odor was the most pungent I ever smelled."

There were signs of animal life in places where the snow had melted away and the ground was soggy. One of the men identified "the footings of deer." Another saw footmarks similar to those of a dog, but Juet was certain they were the prints of a fox. The party picked up a number of deer horns and a piece of whalebone as souvenirs for the captain.

Hudson, waiting on board the *Hopewell*, was entertained by several walruses, which appeared near the ship and cavorted in the water. Peering up the coast, he saw a spot that looked like a walrus landing. He reasoned that if these sea and land beasts found it easy to go ashore there, men might find it convenient, too.

When the party returned in the boat, the captain sent another group ashore to examine the walrus landing. They saw no walruses anywhere near the spot. But they found something far more significant, something man-made. Overcome, they carried it back to the ship. It was a cross, made of two pieces of carved wood, bound by a rawhide thong.

Hudson was deeply moved, and spent a long time examining the cross. Later he wrote in his journal that he believed it had been made and left by Russian hunters. Ducks, geese, and swans were plentiful in the area. So he thought it logical that Russians from the mainland came to the locale in the summer.

Excitement mounted. The men who had not yet gone ashore begged for permission to land. Hudson agreed, and they came back with still more treasures. One carried a bunch of buttercups, "smaller by far than those found in England, but with an odor much sweeter," Hudson wrote. The other members of the party were bareheaded, and the whole company raised a shout when someone called from the boat that the hats were filled with freshly laid birds' eggs, some still warm.

The following morning a large company went ashore, armed with muskets. The men returned in triumph with twenty-four wild geese and another supply of eggs. At Hudson's request, the sailors also brought him samples of moss and grass, which he pressed between the pages of a thick book, intending to take them to Hakluyt.

Walruses continued to appear, and invariably swam off in the direction of the spot Hudson had observed earlier. His curiosity was still piqued. The sea was unusually calm, so he weighed anchor and cautiously sailed to the promontory along the rocky coast. Just past the hill was the mouth of a large "river," with an island several times the size of the *Hopewell* standing guard in the estuary. The ship anchored there, but the current was so strong that she twice slipped from her moorings during the night.

On the morning of June 30 Hudson ordered the company into the boat. Following his directions, the men rowed toward the island, towing the *Hopewell* to a spot unaffected by the current. Huge chunks of ice swept past them out to sea, moving very rapidly.

Hudson threw a square of crimson cloth onto a big ice floe in order to identify it. Then he climbed the rigging into the crow's nest and watched all evening in the perennial daylight. Around midnight the cloth-marked floe finally passed from sight, still moving rapidly. The captain believed the current confirmed the most exciting of all potentials. He was convinced that he was directly opposite the strait he was seeking.

For the present, however, he kept his opinion to himself. He felt it was wrong to raise the men's hopes without first confirming his view. Early the next morning he invited Juet to breakfast and explained his thought. As usual, the mate was pessimistic.

A sudden shout from the lookout brought the entire company to the deck. Twenty walruses had climbed onto a rock jutting out into the sea not far from the island and had gone to sleep in the sun. The tusks of these strange creatures glistened in the sunlight. Hudson knew those tusks were worth a fortune. In the London market they would bring enough to pay the entire costs of the expedition, with a handsome profit left over.

The captain promised the men a share, and the entire crew raced to the boat. Only Hudson and his son remained on board the *Hopewell*. But the walruses proved themselves too clever for the men, and all but one escaped. Deeply chagrined, the seamen explored the island before returning. They killed a large bird and brought back dozens of eggs, but Hudson was still nettled by the loss of the valuable ivory.

He had more important matters on his mind, however. The current was so strong that it ran northward even when the tide flowed to the south. Juet was sent in the boat to investigate. The mouth of the sound was deep and wide, the mate reported. Most important of all, the water flowing from it was salt rather than fresh.

Hudson decided to sail up the "river" of salt water, and an initial attempt was made on the afternoon of July 3. Huge chunks of ice swept down on the *Hopewell*, and the men spent the rest of the day prodding at the floes with spars to prevent damage to the hull.

The current was somewhat less strong on July 4, so Hudson set sail and moved up the "river." It turned out to be a sound, as he had thought. He crossed a reef, and the *Hopewell* now stood in a wide expanse of water. The current, still powerful, flowed through the center in a swift stream. Hudson told the men he believed that, by sailing against the current, they would reach the east coast of Novaya Zemlya. Even Juet agreed.

An east wind blew up. Combined with the current, it was too strong for the *Hopewell*. But Hudson was impatient, and sent Juet out in the boat with five men. The mate was instructed to follow the channel as far as he could.

The men in the bark settled down to wait. At dawn the wind veered to the west, and the captain ordered all hands to man the sails. Come what may, he intended to follow the pilot boat. Before he had sailed more than a short distance, however, the wind shifted again, this time blowing down from the north. The sails were reefed, and again the company waited.

Tension rose. Hudson waved away the food that the cook brought him on the quarterdeck. It was the first meal he had missed since the beginning of the voyage.

At last, early in the afternoon, the boat appeared, sweeping rapidly downstream on the current. One look at the mate's face when Juet came on board the bark was enough to tell Hudson that the news was bad.

The water had grown increasingly shallow, Juet reported. Finally, when there was only four feet of water under his keel, he had been forced to turn back.

Henry Hudson was crushed, his hope of finding a strait that would take him to the eastern shore of Novaya Zemlya blasted. He was tempted to emulate Barents and cross the island on foot. But the idea had no practical value; there would then be no way to proceed by water across the Zara Sea.

Unwilling to admit defeat, he spent several more days cruising up and down the west coast of the island. The weather became unpleasantly cold, the sea was rough, and a rain of hail that froze on the lines made sailing hazardous. But Hudson refused to give up. He remained on the quarterdeck day and night. Trying to salvage what he could of the long voyage, he worked on his charts. It meant little to him, however, that he was drawing the first truly accurate maps of the east coast of Novaya Zemlya that had ever been made.

Hudson paced alone, talking to no one. When he saw a cliff on which hundreds of large birds were resting, he sent the bo's'n ashore with a party, ordering the men to bring back as many as they could shoot. The sailors fired their muskets until they exhausted their ammunition, returning to the *Hopewell* with between one hundred and one hundred and fifty birds.

The cook pronounced the fowl edible. Hudson told him not

to salt the meat. Instead the birds were to be roasted at once, and every man was allowed to eat his fill. That night the crew enjoyed a feast, enlivened by wine from the captain's private store.

Henry Hudson did not join in the merriment. Instead he sat alone in his cabin and wrote a sentence in his log that spelled the seeming end of the adventure. "Tomorrow morning," he said, "we will set sail and stand to the westward, being out of hope to find a passage by the north-east."

At dawn he told the men his decision, and they left the inhospitable shores of Novaya Zemlya behind them. For three days the bark almost flew westward on the current that Hudson had discovered. With time to ponder now, he wrote in his journal that he believed the current to be nothing more than melted snow. As it was warmer than the sea on either side of it, it moved at a faster rate. More than two hundred years would pass before his unique theory would be confirmed.

The crew was overjoyed at the prospect of returning to England after spending three months in the Arctic. They cheered when they saw the characteristically "green water of the main sea." They amused themselves by watching a school of porpoises playing off the starboard bow. The *Hopewell* made such good time that on July 27 she stood off the Lofoten Islands, where sea traffic was so heavy that Hudson ordered a light placed in the binnacle.

Instead of turning southward, however, Hudson continued to sail toward the west. Telling no one his intentions, he planned to head toward the wild coast of Labrador, in far-off North America. He was still thinking and dreaming of the Furious Overfall he had seen on his voyage with John Davys in his youth. If he could find it, if he could discover where it led, he might locate the northwest passage to the Orient. In that event, he would win a glorious triumph. But he knew the men would protest vehemently. So he said nothing to anyone. Even Juet and young John Hudson remained in ignorance.

The idea must have been in Hudson's mind all the time he had been battering in vain at the coast of Novaya Zemlya. Now it became clear why he had relaxed discipline, allowing the men to gorge on wildfowl and drink themselves into stupors on his personal supply of wine. Realizing that the crew would resist a plan to prolong the voyage, he had deliberately distracted them. If all went as he hoped, the bark would reach Greenland before the seamen knew what he had in mind. Then, but only then, would he reveal his audacious scheme.

For several days the sailors remained in the dark. The captain stayed on the quarterdeck himself, and Juet, who was averse to work, made no attempt to relieve him.

Then, on either August 4 or 5, two men who were destined to play major roles in Hudson's future realized what was happening. Michael Perse and Arnold Lodlo compared notes. Both knew the *Hopewell* was sailing west instead of south to England. Rather than confront the captain with their discovery, they went to Juet.

The mate took his own bearings and confirmed the men's guess. Juet said nothing to the captain either. Word spread quickly through the crew, and by August 6 the men were ready to mutiny. They "elected" Juet as their spokesman, and he went to the quarterdeck, accompanied by Perse and Lodlo.

There the trio confronted Henry Hudson. The captain cheerfully admitted he had deceived his crew, saying he had done it "for the benefit and glory of all." The two sailors retired, and Juet pretended he was amenable to Hudson's idea. He voluntarily took the watch, and Hudson went below for his first real sleep in more than a week.

Juet continued to sail on the course that Hudson had ordered him to take. To do otherwise would have ruined his reputation, making it impossible for him to find another berth. But nothing prevented him from conferring freely with the men, who came to the quarterdeck in groups of two and three. John Hudson was the only member of the company who was not consulted by his colleagues.

On the morning of August 7 a demand of some sort was presented to the captain by his crew. No details of the company's request—or ultimatum—have ever been learned. ·

But on that day Hudson wrote an enormously significant entry in his log. "I used all my diligence to arrive at London," he said, "and therefore now I gave my company a certificate under my hand, of my free and willing return, without persuasion or force of any one or more of them."

Obviously there had been serious trouble. It was extraordinary, to say the least, for a ship's master to make any sort of written promise to his men. It was unique for one whose word on his ship was law to explain in such detail that he had not signed the document under duress.

Other captains would have ordered the ringleaders of a conspiracy hanged. Many masters who sailed the seas in the seventeenth century would have run through any sailor who dared to defy the authority of the all-powerful head of the company.

Hudson's wisdom in making his intricate plans secretly and not taking the crew into his confidence is debatable. He was under no obligation to tell the crew his plans. On the other hand, fearing a protest, he might have found it expedient to break the news himself rather than let it leak out. He must have known that, sooner or later, experienced seamen would discover they were sailing west rather than south. And, it appears, he had merely hoped the situation would take care of itself when it finally arose. He gave no indication that he had any specific method of handling the men in mind.

The weakness he displayed when confronted by a mutiny, however, was contrary to the basic principles of the sea. It was a captain's first duty to command. Henry Hudson's personal courage was unquestioned. His passion for discovery was as great as that of any explorer who ever lived. His seamanship was superb, and he repeatedly demonstrated true genuis as an explorer. Nevertheless, on August 7, 1608, he revealed an inability to handle men in a moment of supreme crisis.

The dispute between him and the crew of the *Hopewell* simmered down on the homeward voyage. Amicable relations were restored, and the incident was forgotten by the time the bark reached Gravesend, England, on August 26. Perhaps the sailors were afraid they would be punished for their temerity if the news leaked out. Perhaps the captain was ashamed of the weakness he had shown. Whatever the reasons, no mention was made of the unpleasant incident.

IV

The Jolly Burghers

CROWDS GATHERED to cheer Henry Hudson in the streets of
London when he returned from his second voyage. He received a perfunctory invitation to pay his respects to King
James, and in mid-September was received in a brief, formal
audience. Then he was promptly forgotten by his fellow
countrymen.

Only Archdeacon Hakluyt, echoed by the Reverend Samuel
Purchas, realized the significance of Hudson's second great
voyage. In a sense, the results had been negative. Hudson had
proved that there was no northeast passage to the Orient. He
had returned with excellent new maps of Novaya Zemlya
that would be of great help to the explorers who came after
him. But it was impossible for him—or any other man—to meet
the greatest challenge of his era.

The factors of the Muscovy Company lost all interest in
trying to find a short sea route to Cathay. They wanted to

make money and cared nothing about discovery for its own sake. They were already showing a handsome profit from their whaling expeditions to Spitsbergen, and wrote off Novaya Zemlya. They also wrote off Henry Hudson. He was summoned to a directors' meeting, thanked for his services, and peremptorily dismissed.

Hudson himself felt he had failed. Hakluyt tried to disabuse him of the idea, in person and in correspondence, but could not. Samuel Purchas later claimed he had met Hudson several times in the autumn of 1608 and had found the explorer "sunk into the lowest depths of the Humor of Melancholy, from which no man could rouse him. It mattered not that his Perseverance and Industry had made England the richer by his maps of the North. I told him he had created Fame that would endure for all time, but he would not listen to me."

Hudson did not brood for long. At some time in the autumn of 1608 he received a visit from Emanuel van Meteran, for many years the Dutch Consul in London, who also acted as the English representative of the Dutch East India Company. On that occasion Van Meteran casually reminded his host that the Dutch merchants had offered the staggering sum of two thousand five hundred gold florins to the man who discovered a new, short route to the Orient, be it by east or west.

Somewhat to the Dutchman's surprise, Hudson showed little interest in the prize. Perhaps it meant nothing to him because he lacked the funds to finance an expedition of his own. At least that was what Van Meteran gleaned. Soon afterward the explorer was invited to dine at the Dutch Consulate. There, over steaming dumplings seasoned with spices from the East, Van Meteran dangled a bait. He had friends in Amsterdam who believed in the future of Henry Hudson. Would the Englishman care to meet them?

Hudson expressed no objection. So, in November, the Consul presented him with a formal letter. The factors of the Dutch East India Company were pleased to request the honor of meeting Captain Hudson at their main offices, and would be happy to pay all expenses he would incur on his journey.

The invitation was accepted but was delayed for personal reasons. Hudson had to attend the christening of his first grandchild, Alice, the daughter of Oliver Hudson, at the church of St. Mary Aldermary in London. The happy family occasion undoubtedly made him feel his age. When a man first becomes a grandfather he inevitably realizes that the years are passing swiftly.

Hudson was in a dour mood when he sailed for Holland on a commercial cross-Channel packet boat. The sea was rough, the ship tiny, and the conqueror of the Arctic almost disgraced himself. "The odors below deck were so offensive to my nostrils," he wrote to Katherine, "that I begged the captain for the privilege of standing on his quarterdeck so I would not become ill."

Certainly Hudson understood why he had been summoned to the Netherlands. The Dutch, with typical industry, were forging one of the strongest and wealthiest commercial empires on earth. Their explorers had been diligent, fearless men, and had established thriving trade relations with Far East islanders in the realm that was destined to become the Dutch East Indies and, eventually, the independent nation of Indonesia.

The Staats-General, or Dutch Parliament, was very much aware of the weaknesses in English mercantile policy. Charters were granted by the English Crown to various groups of English investors, who thereafter operated on their own, financing their operations out of their own pockets. Some of these companies were rivals, with clashing interests. And all suffered from an occasional inability to raise enough money to pay for their expeditions of exploration.

Profiting by these mistakes, the Staats-General established an organization that was unique. In 1602 the Dutch East India Company was formed. Powerful merchants, among them Balthasar de Moucheron and Isaac Le Maire, were directors. All competing Dutch groups were included in this one company. And the Staats-General itself was represented. National funds could be voted by the Staats-General to augment the investments made by individual directors. Hence, for all practical purposes, the Dutch East India Company was an arm of the government. And, relatively speaking, its resources were unlimited.

Its offer of a rich prize to anyone who found a new, short route to the Orient was typical of its operations. It was alert, aggressive and the most farsighted of all the many European groups fighting for trade and the establishment of colonies all over the globe.

Henry Hudson knew that the directors were interested in acquiring his services. If he could make a mutually satisfactory arrangement, he had no reason to hesitate on nationalistic grounds. For more than one hundred years it had been the policy of England and every Continental power to hire foreign explorers. At the very time he made his journey to Holland, several Danes and Swedes were in the employ of the shrewd Henry IV of France. A number of Englishmen were in the pay of Portugal, and at least two Norwegians were accepting wages from English companies. Custom prohibited a man only from accepting work from his nation's enemies. Thus no

Englishman would work for Spain, and no Spaniard would accept employment from the English. In all other respects, a man was free to make any deal he could.

The directors of the Dutch East India Company were in no hurry to receive Hudson, and let him cool his heels in Amsterdam. Perhaps it was their intention to soften him and thus obtain better terms. But a man who had traveled through the Arctic and had spent years sailing the Atlantic was not interested in sightseeing. Instead he went to The Hague, where he spent a week as the house guest of the Reverend Peter Plancius, the only geographer on earth who was Richard Hakluyt's equal.

There was an immediate rapport. Hudson's knowledge of Dutch was limited, as was Plancius' ability to speak English. Therefore they communicated in Latin, a fact that proves Hudson had received far more than an ordinary education in his youth. The Dutch geographer and the English explorer spent hours poring over maps, exchanging information, and expounding theories on the true nature of the world in which they lived.

They were kindred spirits, of course. Hudson felt as much at home with Plancius as he did with Hakluyt or Purchas. Plancius saw in Hudson the English counterpart of Barents and Jacob van Heemskerk. Explorers had similar temperaments, and great geographers were alike, too.

Plancius, reminiscing about their talks in later correspondence, observed that Hudson spoke of little except his desire to find a new passage to Cathay. He had lived with the idea for so long that it had become an obsession. Plancius said that Hudson's eyes glowed when he traced possible routes on a map with the point of his dagger. Like all members of his profession, discovery meant everything to him.

The conversations were interrupted by a message from Amsterdam. The directors of the Dutch East India Company had gathered and were awaiting Captain Hudson's pleasure.

Hudson rode to Amsterdam on a horse he borrowed from Plancius. His first impression of the directors was that they were very reserved men. They said little, and he did most of the talking. He needed no encouragement.

It was his firm opinion, he told them, that a route to the East could be found over the roof of the world. His failures at Spitsbergen and Novaya Zemlya had only served to whet his appetite for exploration. He produced more than a score of maps and charts, and "proved" his theories—to his own satisfaction.

The directors listened carefully. After all, Hudson had made two long voyages to the Arctic, and deserved to be heard with respect. Unknown to him, the directors were in possession of a report from a Dutch navigator who was similarly convinced that the seas were open near the North Pole and that the weather there was balmy.

The case that Hudson made seemed good. But the directors were businessmen who had to deal in hard, known facts. Meeting privately while their guest retired to quarters at an inn, they discussed his suggestion for several hours. The powerful La Maire was inclined to take a chance on Hudson, and influenced several others to vote with him. The majority were opposed.

Nothing could be done, however, without getting an opinion from de Moucheron, who disdainfully refused to attend directors' meetings. So a letter was sent to him at his quiet country home, presenting both sides of the argument. De Moucheron read the communication, walked in his rose garden, and played with his pet dogs. Forty-eight hours later he scribbled a reply on the bottom of the last sheet of parchment in the directors' letter to him.

"Master Hudson's plans are not a good investment for the Dutch East India Company," he wrote. The deciding ballot was now cast.

Hudson was called in again, and the directors handled him with great tact and deft diplomacy. They had no desire to make an enemy of him by curtly rejecting his scheme. It was unfortunate, they said, that several members of the Staats-General could not be present. No final decision could be made without these gentlemen. The next regularly scheduled meeting would be held on March 25, 1609, and by that time it would be too late to send an expedition to the Arctic in the same year.

Therefore, they told Hudson, no action could be taken for several months. They assured him, warmly but vaguely, that they hoped to have employment for him by spring. And they made him a gift of five pounds in silver to pay for his traveling expenses, food, and lodging.

Hudson immediately returned to The Hague, seemingly undismayed by the polite dismissal. It was apparent in his conversations with Peter Plancius that the directors had not fooled him. He well knew they had no intention of financing a new expedition to the Arctic. He did not blame them, he said.

Then, behind the closed door of the geographer's study, he confided a secret of his own, a secret he was willing to tell a fellow scientist but would not reveal to mere men of commerce. He had no intention of going to the Arctic again, in either 1609 or any other year. Instead, he intended to find the northwest sea passage to Cathay. He was convinced the Furious Overfall would lead him to it.

Plancius had heard rumors of the Furious Overfall, but had no detailed information. Hudson, who had seen the Overfall with his own eyes, filled him in. More than that, the captain drew maps of the Labrador coast of North America to substantiate his theory that somewhere along the coast was a broad channel. That channel, he said, opened from the Atlantic Ocean onto the Pacific.

His maps, drawn freehand, were remarkably accurate. Plancius kept them as souvenirs of his meeting with a man whom he considered more gifted than either of his two great pupils, Barents and Heemskerk, who had carried the Dutch flag into so many previously unknown quarters of the globe.

Hudson also revealed that he was no simpleton. He had guessed from the outset that the directors of the Dutch East India Company had hoped he would reveal all he knew and believed about the earth and seas of the world. But he said he would not divulge such information to them, any more than he would tell it to the factors of the Muscovy Company in London.

The theory that a North American channel or strait connected the Atlantic and Pacific seemed logical to Plancius. In fact, the idea coincided with some of his own privately held views. He was excited by the realization that he and Hudson had reached similar conclusions independently of each other.

Now the question arose: what was to be done?

The geographer felt no more loyalty to Holland in the matter than Hudson felt to England. Exploration, in the minds of these scientific experts, knew no national borders. Plancius weighed the problem at length, then discussed it with Hudson. They agreed that the theory of the Furious Overfall should be tested by an actual expedition. Yet they shared the fear that public disclosure of their views might set off a wild race in which seafarers of a dozen nations might take part. Hudson's rights had to be protected.

Plancius finally determined to play a game worthy of the most devious minds of the Middle Ages, much less of the Renaissance in which he lived. Dutch and English seamen were the most competent; the French were good enough, the Scandinavians allegedly headstrong and unreliable. There could be no dealings with Spain. The Dutch had only recently won a war against England's archenemy, Philip II, and feeling against the Spaniards still ran high. Therefore, by a process of elimination, Plancius decided the expedition should be financed by either the English or the Dutch. Hudson told him there was no interest in London mercantile circles, so that left the Dutch East India Company.

Plancius baited his hook with care, using France as his bait. Henry IV, popularly known as Henry of Navarre, was achieving near-miracles in uniting his country, encouraging agriculture and industry, and building a strong navy. Of all Europe's monarchs, he had the liveliest interest in North America and the greatest appreciation of the continent's colonial potential. French explorers, subsidized by the Crown, were already making epic journeys up the St. Lawrence River and down the Mississippi. On several occasions French emissaries had come to Plancius with offers of impressive monetary gifts in return for any knowledge of value he cared to impart.

The geographer felt that if he got in touch with the French, he would be obligated to them. That was not his intention. Therefore it was better to find some way to bring the French to him, seemingly of their own accord.

With Hudson's consent, Plancius now brought Isaac Le Maire into the plot. The merchant was told no details, but was merely informed that a great scheme was in the making. Hudson's strongest supporter on the board of the East India Company was willing to do everything within his power, but could not compromise his own position as a director of the Dutch company.

After a delay of a few days, the merchant's brother, Jacob Le Maire, wrote an innocuous letter to one of King Henry's closest friends and stanchest supporters, Pierre Jeannin, the wily old President of the Parliament of Burgundy. The letter has not survived, but whatever Jacob Le Maire may have written brought Jeannin to The Hague in a hurry.

Jacob held a meeting with him and told him it was rumored that Henry Hudson, the noted English explorer, might be available. Jacob added he had been told on good authority that Hudson's deal with the Dutch East India Company had collapsed. Jeannin wanted direct confirmation, so Hudson, acting his role cleverly, met the distinguished Burgundian briefly. It was true, Hudson said, that as yet he had acquired no sponsor for a forthcoming expedition. He said nothing more, and retired into seclusion at Plancius' house.

Naturally Jeannin then went to Plancius, who admitted that he and the English captain were working together on a project. Jacob Le Maire reentered the scene and told Jeannin that he wanted a share of any project sponsored by the French. Jeannin agreed, and wrote a long letter to King Henry, urging that funds be advanced from the French national treasury for the project.

Jacob asked for a copy of the letter, signed by Jeannin, to protect his interests. Jeannin gave it to him, and when it was shown to Hudson and Plancius, they must have been surprised at how much the Burgundian had surmised.

"It will be pleasing to Your Majesty's ear," Jeannin wrote, "that Hudson believes he will soon discover a short passage to the Indies. It is said everywhere that he and Plancius stand agreed on the route he will take. The talents of these men are formidable.

"The whole voyage, both out and home, can be finished in six months without approaching any of the harbors or fortresses of the King of Spain; whilst by the road round the Cape of Good Hope, which is now in common use, one generally requires three years and one is besides exposed to meet and fight the Portuguese.

"Hudson will sail in no ship that does not meet his own requirements. That Your Majesty has many ships suitable for the purpose is a certainty. Jacob Le Maire, of whom I have already spoken to Your Majesty in this letter, believes that an additional sum of four thousand crowns, in gold, must be spent to prepare a ship for such a voyage. He does not know what wages Hudson will require. Nor does he know whether Hudson would sail with a French crew. Nor do I."

There was one more thread in the intricate net that Plancius was weaving. He consented to meet Jeannin again, and innocently confirmed his own conviction that a route to the Orient could be found by way of the North Pole. This information was duly communicated to King Henry, and the secret of the Furious Overfall, shared only by Plancius and Hudson, was duly protected.

Now the hook was baited, and Hudson left Plancius' house to take up lodgings with Jodocus Hondius, one of the most colorful figures in the whole network of plot and counterplot. Hondius, one of the most celebrated sculptors, metalworkers, and engravers of his age, was noted for his bronze statues. One of his most famous was that of Alexander Farnese, the great warrior Duke of Parma. At one point in his life he had visited

England, where he had engraved portraits of Sir Francis Drake and other national heroes.

It is possible that he may have become friendly with Hudson on that visit. In any event, they knew each other sufficiently well for Hudson to pass the time by giving Hondius full details of his voyages to the Arctic. He supervised the drawing of the map that Hondius made of the Far North. That map, when published, was to bring Hondius greater fame than all of his statues.

During Hudson's stay with Hondius he received a letter from a close friend who had just returned to England from Jamestown, in the Colony of Virginia, which he had helped to establish. Captain John Smith believed Hudson could find his short route to the Pacific somewhere north of Virginia. Himself an excellent cartographer, he sent along a number of maps he had made to prove his contention.

The maps, based in large part on the hearsay evidence given Smith by Indians, suggest that he thought of the Great Lakes as a single body of salt water running in a continuous channel across the entire North American continent. Neither the intrepid captain nor anyone else dreamed that the continent might be more than a few hundred miles wide.

That Smith should have sent Hudson the letter and maps indicates there was a bond that tied the discoverer-adventurers of the Renaissance to each other. Birds of a feather flocked closely together in a brotherhood. Hondius, the friend of Drake, copied the maps drawn by Smith, the friend of Hudson!

The interlude at Hondius' house must have been pleasant for Henry Hudson, but his days of waiting were almost ended. Isaac Le Maire, armed with the copy of Jeannin's letter given to his brother, went to his fellow directors of the Dutch East

India Company in pretended alarm. Here, he said, was absolute proof that the King of France would offer to sponsor Hudson's next voyage. If the route across the North Pole should be discovered, Paris would become the capital of the world. Amsterdam's trade with the islands of the Far East would shrink, and she would become just another dreary, provincial town.

The alarmed directors agreed that this must not be allowed to happen. An urgent letter was sent to Hudson at The Hague, asking him to return to Amsterdam at his earliest convenience for consultations.

Hudson and Plancius knew they had won the battle. But they thought it wise for the explorer not to appear overly eager. Hudson sent a short note to Dirk Van Os, managing director of the company, saying it would suit his convenience to visit Amsterdam after he had celebrated the beginning of the new year, then four days distant, at The Hague.

Early in January, 1609, he went to Amsterdam, taking Hondius with him as his interpreter. He believed that hard bargaining was in store, and wanted his own interpreter rather than one provided by the company.

The directors were in no mood to quibble. Rather than run the risk of losing the Englishman to King Henry, they agreed to all his demands. Only in the matter of his own personal wages was Hudson indifferent. In fact, he was so eager to make his new voyage that he agreed to accept a small fraction of what he could have asked.

The document read:

Contract With Henry Hudson

On this eighth day of January in the year of our Lord one thousand six hundred and nine, the Directors of the East India

Company of the Chamber of Amsterdam of the ten years reckoning of the one part, and Mr. Henry Hudson, Englishman, assisted by Jodocus Hondius, of the other part, have agreed in manner following, to wit:

That the said directors shall in the first place equip a small vessel or yacht of about thirty lasts burden, with which, well provided with men, provisions and other necessaries, the above named Hudson shall about the first of April, sail, in order to search for a passage by the North, around by the North side of Nova Zembla, and shall continue thus along that parallel until he shall be able to sail Southward to the latitude of sixty degrees.

He shall obtain as much knowledge of the lands as can be done without any considerable loss of time, and if it is possible return immediately in order to make a faithful report and relation of his voyage to the directors, and to deliver over his journals, log-books and charts, together with an account of everything whatsoever which shall happen to him during the voyage without keeping anything back; for which said voyage the directors shall pay to the said Hudson, as well as for his outfit for the said voyage, as for the support of his wife and children, the sum of eight hundred guilders; and in case, which God prevent, he do not come back or arrive hereabouts within one year, the directors shall further pay to his wife two hundred guilders in silver; and thereupon they shall not be further liable to him or his heirs, unless he shall either afterwards or within the year arrive and have found the passage good and suitable for the Company to use; in which case the directors will reward the before-named Hudson for his dangers, trouble and knowledge in their discretion, with which the before-named Hudson is content.

And in case the directors think proper to prosecute and

continue the same voyage, it is stipulated and agreed with the before-named Hudson, that he shall make his residence in this country wtih his wife and children, and shall enter into the employment of no one other than the Company, and at the isfied and content for such further service in all justice and discretion of the directors, who also promise to make him sat-equity.

All without fraud or evil intent.

In witness of the truth, two contracts are made hereof of the same tenor and are subscribed by both parties and also by Jodocus Hondius, as interpreter and witness.

Dated as above,

> *Dirk Van Os*
> *J. Poppe*
> *Henry Hudson*
> *Jodocus Hondius, witness*

None of the signers could have imagined the consequences of the voyage Henry Hudson was now contracted to make.

In itself, the document was remarkable. In the first place, Hudson had no intention of keeping his agreement. He had already promised himself never to search for the North Pole route to the Orient, and was planning to find out where the Furious Overfall led. In the second place, his bland agreement to live in Holland with his wife and children was of dubious legality, to say the least. All three of his sons were of age, and consequently were not bound by any promise made by their father. Presumably Hudson was within his rights to tell his wife where she would or would not live. But, as Katherine would have been obliged to dwell in a foreign land, an English court well might have ruled the clause invalid. It appears that Hudson did not take any of his contractual obligations very seriously.

He returned to The Hague immediately after signing the contract, and there held a final, private meeting with Peter Plancius. In later correspondence with Hakluyt, Plancius declared that he tried to persuade Hudson to live up to the letter of the contract. He also said that, in his opinion, a northern passage could be found, but a western passage could not.

Having done his duty, Plancius removed from his strongbox some exceptionally valuable papers. They were the journals of George Weymouth, the Englishman who had been in command of the last important voyage to the northwest. Weymouth, a meticulous seaman, had kept a detailed, accurate account of his route, together with his personal impressions of climate and the nature of the sea.

Hudson made a brief journey to England. He read Weymouth's journals en route, and almost immediately after reaching London wrote a guarded letter to Plancius. "The notes that you placed in my safekeeping," he said, "are worth more than gold and silver."

Katherine Hudson's reaction to her husband's new venture is not known. By now she must have become accustomed to his frequent voyages. It is also safe to assume that she felt familiar disappointment over his financial arrangements.

The first man Hudson signed to accompany him was Robert Juet, the mate who had been disloyal to him on his last voyage! The captain must have known that Juet had conspired with the mutineers. Why he wanted Juet to accompany him again is an unsolved mystery. Perhaps the mate was so glib and clever that he persuaded Hudson he had not taken a disloyal role in the mutiny. No other explanation makes sense.

Hudson also sought out John Colman, his mate on his first voyage. Colman had earned a considerable sum in whaling during the past year, and was once again yearning for adventure. When he learned Hudson's true destination, which the captain told both him and Juet in secrecy, Colman could not resist the lure. He signed as second mate.

It would have been absurd to carry three mates on a small ship, but John Hudson wanted to go with his father again, too. The captain solved the problem by listing his son on his manifest as a passenger.

Hudson returned at once to Amsterdam, the others following him in mid-February. Before his departure he hired "several" English sailors, but nowhere did he keep a list of their number or names. Dutch laws were less strict than English laws, which may account for the fact that no record of the names of the crew was maintained.

As soon as Hudson reached Amsterdam he became involved in a heated argument with the directors of the Dutch East India Company. Van Os balked at paying the high wages Hudson had agreed to give his mates and English seamen. The captain stood firm. His own contract was ambiguous on the point, so neither side had a legal advantage. But Hudson threatened to call off the whole deal, and the directors were forced to capitulate.

Even Isaac Le Maire, Hudson's champion, was moved to write Van Os, "If he rebels here, under our eyes, what will he do when he is away from us?"

Perhaps the question was rhetorical, reflecting a general sense of uneasiness on the part of directors dealing with a stubborn foreigner. On the other hand, rumors were circulating freely in London to the effect that Hudson had no intention of trying to sail across the North Pole again. Apparently Juet and Colman, unable to keep the great secret entrusted to them, were being indiscreet. The whispers may have carried across the North Sea to Amsterdam; if so, La

Maire, Van Os, and the others had good reason to feel apprehensive.

They could prove nothing, of course. Hudson continued to talk and act as though he intended to obey the letter of his agreement. But they knew that, once he put to sea, he would be his own master, that nothing they might say now would deter him from setting his own course.

A year later, in London, Juet declared that the Dutch East India Company operated on a very strict budget and that, having been compelled to pay higher wages than anticipated, the directors gave their captain an old, inferior ship rather than building him a new one. The charge may have been valid. Even in an era of tiny seagoing craft, the vessel they assigned Hudson was not impressive.

Her name was the *Half Moon*, and her gross weight was a scant sixty tons. She was strangely old-fashioned in appearance, riding high in the water like the flat-bottomed boats the Dutch used in their inland waterway, the Zuider Zee. Her poop and fo'c'sle were higher than those of comparable English ships, her three masts looked thin, and Hudson's initial reaction was that she would prove clumsy.

"I fear," he wrote La Maire in a brief letter of complaint, "that she will prove difficult to handle in foul weather."

Her quarters were cramped, too, and the master's suite of cabins was smaller than Hudson had enjoyed on his previous voyages. He decided his two mates would have to share a cabin in order that the space thus saved could be utilized as his private galley. He was being neither selfish nor inconsiderate in assigning himself enlarged quarters at the expense of his junior officers, however. The customs of the times made it necessary for a ship's master to remain aloof. Therefore he was required to eat his meals alone, inviting others to join him only on rare and special occasions.

Scraps of evidence suggest that Hudson tried to obtain a newer and larger ship. He remembered the swift current of the Furious Overfall, and wanted to be prepared for a rough voyage into the unknown. But the directors proved to him that the Dutch could be as stubborn as an Englishman. Van Os became tired of the captain's persistent demands, and wrote him a curt note:

"The *Half Moon* is the only ship at the disposal of the Dutch East India Company. If you read your contract again, you will see that we are living up to our bargain. We can give you no other ship. If you do not want the *Half Moon*, the Company will be obliged to find another Captain to carry out this assignment."

By now Van Os knew his man, and was taking only a slight gamble. Plans were so far advanced that Hudson, anxious to make the voyage, probably would not withdraw at this late date. Van Os proved himself right; although Hudson continued to grumble, he finally accepted the vessel.

The Dutch members of the crew were strangers to the captain, and hiring them must have been a difficult and ticklish procedure. Hudson's command of the Dutch language was limited, and prospective seamen for the *Half Moon*'s voyage knew no English. Therefore Hudson was forced to rely on his friend, Jodocus Hondius, as an interpreter. Hondius may have been one of the great mapmakers and artists of his time, but he certainly was no sailor. Life before the mast was unknown to him. He had never paced a quarterdeck, and on the few occasions he had gone to sea, he had been a passenger who had not participated in the operations of the vessel. Nothing in his background indicated that he was qualified as a judge of character, either.

Nevertheless, Hudson was forced to depend on him. By the time Juet and Colman reached Holland, the entire crew had been hired, and the mates were not impressed. "They are an ugly lot," Juet wrote in his diary.

Colman was even more specific in a letter to his wife. "I hope," he said, "that these square-faced men know the sea. Looking at their fat bellies, I fear they think more highly of eating than of sailing."

From the outset, then, there was friction between the officers and the majority of the crew. Other minor squabbles also marred the weeks of preparation for the voyage. English seamen were accustomed to rations of beef, and would have mutinied had they not been served the meat they considered their due. Dutch seamen, on the other hand, seemed content to subsist almost exclusively on herring. The British did not object to an occasional meal of herring, but were horrified when they saw their Dutch colleagues carry barrel after barrel of salted fish into the hold.

Hudson tried to mollify his countrymen by purchasing adequate quantities of beef for them, but he immediately ran into snags. Pickled beef was considered a luxury in Holland, and prices were exorbitant, even when the beef was purchased by the barrel. The captain promptly appealed to the company for more funds. The exasperated directors rejected his request, refusing to listen to him.

Hudson solved the dilemma in his own way by going to the markets of Amsterdam in person, ordering what he wanted, and blithely sending the bills to Van Os. The meat was stowed in the hold, and the captain turned a deaf ear when the outraged directors screamed that he was exceeding his authority.

The English members of the crew protested again when they learned that their cook would be a Dutchman. Even the officers were apprehensive, and Colman wrote to his wife, "Men have been known to die of slow poisoning at sea when fed by a foreign cook." Even in the early seventeenth century, Englishmen clung tenaciously to their own methods of preparing food.

Hudson was in a position to find out for himself whether the food the cook would prepare on the voyage would be edible. He ordered dinner served to him on board about ten days before sailing, and was both surprised and delighted by the unexpected results. "The Captain," Juet scribbled in his diary, "swears that he has never tasted finer edibles. But," he added darkly, "I wonder if he tells the truth."

More important matters occupied the major part of Hudson's attention, however. As the *Half Moon* was old, small, and might prove untrustworthy in a storm, he ordered every inch of sail and every foot of line tested. As an added precaution he had spare masts cut and stored in the hold, and a few days before leaving decided he wanted a spare set of sails, too.

In spite of the innumerable tragedies caused at sea by the loss of sails, ships did not carry spare sets. The directors' patience was exhausted, and Hudson was informed that if he wanted extra sails, he would have to pay for them out of his own pocket. Again he resorted to the stratagem of charging his purchases, and Van Os was so furiously angry that he refused to attend a farewell dinner given by Plancius in the captain's honor.

Word of the incessant bickering reached London, and the reports were so inflated as they swept across the North Sea that English gentlemen were offering wagers at two-to-one odds that the *Half Moon* would not leave port. Even seamen sufficiently experienced to realize that the difficulties were minor predicted that trouble was brewing and that Hudson, the English master of a Dutch ship, would find it impossible to impose discipline on a crew made up in the main of foreigners.

A final incident was far more serious than the petty arguments that had marred relations between the officials of the Dutch East India Company and their distinguished English employee. The directors wanted Hudson to sail in March, explaining that they believed his chances of finding an Arctic passage to the Orient would be enhanced if he started very early in the spring. Hudson refused, saying it was too early, that the northern seas would still be filled with "islands of ice" which would unnecessarily jeopardize his ship and crew.

The directors insisted that he go in March, and Van Os wrote him a strong letter, commanding him to set sail "no later than the fifteenth day of March."

A forceful commander might have retorted that he had been given responsibility and that his duty to his men and his ship compelled him to rely on his own judgment. Hudson, however, chose to handle the situation with typical guile. He accepted the order, but privately made up his mind not to obey it. Then he utilized the simple ruse of delaying his final preparations, deliberately slowing the pace of his last-minute arrangements, but protesting to the directors that events beyond his control were making it impossible for him to leave on schedule.

On the first day of April, a warm breeze blew in from the west across the Dutch lowlands, belatedly heralding the arrival of spring. The last vestiges of ice and snow vanished from the cobblestones of Amsterdam's streets, and the next morning crocuses appeared miraculously in hundreds of householders' gardens.

Equally miraculously, Henry Hudson's problems seemed to melt away overnight, and he announced that he was ready to sail at once. His bo's'n, a Dutchman, hurriedly rounded up the crew, and the captain made ready to depart.

But there were new, last-minute delays, and this time the Dutch East India Company was responsible. The directors had obtained evidence which, if not conclusive, at least proved to their own satisfaction that the troublesome Englishman had no intention of trying to find a sea passage to the east by way of the North Pole. In some inexplicable manner they had ferreted out his plan to sail west by way of the Americas.

An emergency meeting was held, and Hudson was summoned to appear before the directors. Van Os presented the charges, bristling indignantly. Hudson, equally angry, denied them. Apparently his ability to play-act left something to be desired, and he was asked to attend still another meeting two days later.

He returned to his lodgings, fuming, and spent forty-eight hours doing nothing. But the directors were busy, and devised a scheme they considered foolproof. When Hudson came before them again, they demanded that he swear an oath on the Bible that he would attempt the Polar passage.

He had no alternative, and therefore agreed. Had the directors been a trifle shrewder, they might have wondered at his readiness to accept the conditions they imposed on him. They believed, rightly, that he would not disavow a sworn pledge. What they failed to take into consideration was the astute cunning of the man with whom they were dealing.

Hudson had been waiting for a lifetime to test his theory

that he could reach the Orient by sailing westward. The men who had hired him could not stop him from trying to attain his goal, nor could be he dissuaded by the oath they had forced him to swear under pressure. Perhaps he had anticipated their action, for he was ready, instantly, with a counterscheme. He intended to let nothing stand between him and his goal. At the height of his powers as a mariner, at the peak of his reputation, he was prepared to overcome any obstacle as he put his grand design into operation.

V

The Half Moon

ॐ

THE MIST OF CENTURIES obscures the details of the *Half Moon*'s departure from Holland. But enough is known to make one fact clear. Few voyages had ever begun less auspiciously. There was no fanfare and no ceremony. The directors of the Dutch East India Company, annoyed with Henry Hudson, did not appear to wish him Godspeed. If the captain and his crew attended a religious service, no record of the event has survived. Perhaps the wives and children of the Dutch seamen gathered to wave farewell to their loved ones. But Hudson's friends were not on hand, for Hondius wrote a note to Plancius on April 8, saying, "I have heard that Hudson began his adventure two days ago."

From the outset, the weather itself seemed to conspire against the master of the tiny vessel—and against his ship. Only a few hours after the vessel nosed out into the North Sea on April 6, 1609, the balmy breezes dried up, the bright sun

79

disappeared behind thick banks of clouds, and a gale shrieked down out of the northwest.

The *Half Moon* creaked and groaned ominously as the unexpected storm struck her. The sailors had not yet had time to get their "sea legs," and several disgraced themselves by becoming so ill that they collapsed in their hammocks. Juet contemptuously noted in his diary that John Hudson was badly frightened, an allegation that may or may not have been true. Juet hated the captain so intensely that he may have taken out his spite on Hudson's son. Although the mate's observations on most subjects were reliable, his loathing for the master was so intense it clouded his vision and warped his judgment. Why he had consented to sail with a man for whom he felt such hatred is an impenetrable mystery.

But the crew quickly learned the true character of their captain. In all, approximately eighteen to twenty men sailed with Hudson; the exact number has never been determined. Of these, perhaps fifteen were fit for duty, and all were summoned to their stations when the storm struck.

Unlike other masters of the day, many of whom were petty tyrants, Hudson was remarkably gentle. He gave an order just once, but expected to be obeyed promptly and efficiently. He corrected errors swiftly, wasting no words.

In a very short time he demonstrated to his crew that he was a superb sailor. He knew precisely how to handle a ship in rough seas, and even the lumbering *Half Moon* responded to his touch. He understood winds and tides, and seemed to possess a sixth sense, an instinct that enabled him to anticipate how an erratic storm would behave.

Lashed to the quarterdeck rail, he held the vessel on course all afternoon and through the long hours of the night. He gave his commands in English, but the Dutch seamen managed to understand him. By dawn, when the weather began to clear, Englishmen and Dutchmen had learned to work together under the direction of a master who set an example by cheerfully remaining at his post until the high winds subsided and the sea became calmer.

Hudson quietly noted in his log that the experience had been beneficial to all hands. "My men," he wrote, "now act as though they had been sailing together for many years."

With the gale behind him, the captain was able to think in terms of the future. He must have been tempted to sail toward the New World at once, but he had taken an oath and could not forget it. So he obediently set his course for the Arctic. What he intended to do thereafter was something that, apparently, he told no one. Certainly he had good reason not to trust the discretion of Juet and Colman.

The *Half Moon* sluggishly made her way up the coast of Norway, the third time that Hudson had followed the identical course. Finally, on May 5, a full month after leaving Holland, the North Cape was sighted. The weather was even colder than the captain had anticipated, and everyone suffered. Sailors were unable to climb into the rigging for more than half an hour at a time without running the grave risk of freezing.

Some of the Dutch seamen seemed particularly vulnerable to the bitter cold, and when Hudson learned the reason he must have cursed his friend, Hondius, who had conducted only a superficial interrogation of prospective members of the expedition. Now, when it was too late, Hudson discovered that the majority of the sailors had seen long service in the tropical waters of the East Indies. Unaccustomed to cold, they were miserable.

Their lack of acclimatization to the Arctic may have been

the basic cause of the troubles that erupted during the next two weeks. Hudson's log and journal contain only vague references to difficulties. Even the usually verbose Juet kept his thoughts to himself and did not set them down in his diary. It may be that the captain and his first mate were too busy trying to bring a mutiny under control to spend much time with pen in hand.

Accounts of the voyage written in later years by both Dutch and English historians who had opportunities to confer with Hudson indicate that the Dutch and English sailors who had worked so well together now split into two foul-tempered, opposing camps. The causes of the bad feeling were simple. The thin-blooded Dutchmen avoided unpleasant outdoor chores whenever possible, using the flimsiest of excuses to huddle near the wood-burning stoves in the galley.

Consequently the burden of dirty work fell on the Englishmen, who were compelled to do more than their fair share. They chopped ice from pulleys, kneaded frozen sails and lines with their bare hands, cleared the rudder with axes attached to long poles, and swept ever accumulating snow from the quarterdeck. A few days of carrying these extra burdens created an explosive situation. The English considered the Dutch lazy and irresponsible.

Heated words were exchanged, fists flew, and spars were used as clubs. Colman allegedly averted bloodshed by sneaking into the seamen's sleeping quarters while they were at dinner in the galley and quietly confiscating their knives and other personal weapons.

A condition of near-anarchy prevailed on board the *Half Moon.* A harsh captain would have hung the ringleaders of both disputing parties and restored peace. But Henry Hudson once again demonstrated his strange inability to handle violent mutineers. Apparently he spent several days going from one group to the other, pleading for greater tolerance and understanding. His efforts did not end the feud, but at least no murders were committed.

The weather was particularly bad on Tuesday, May 19. Snow, whipped by an icy wind, cut across the open deck of the ship, and it was impossible for the men to keep warm indoors, even when they gathered around the stove. Then, for a short time, the clouds blew away and a strange phenomenon was noted in the sky. The men saw a sunspot, and Juet made history by recording the observation in his diary. It was the first time that a sunspot had ever been mentioned on paper. Juet called it a "slake," which, in the slang of the period, meant a mound or accumulation of dirt.

The sailors were deeply impressed, and Hudson, who had been awaiting a propitious moment, called a meeting of the entire crew.

It is possible, even probable, that he had been cunning rather than merely weak when he had allowed the feud to rage unchecked. He had maneuvered the men into an untenable position, and in view of his determination to sail to the New World, it is unlikely that he achieved mastery of the situation by accident.

The sailors were frightened by the sunspot, and several were afraid the world was coming to an end. For the moment, at least, differences between Dutchmen and Englishmen were forgotten.

The captain delivered a pungent address, building carefully and logically to his climax. Differences of opinion in the fo'c'-sle, he declared, made it difficult to continue the northern voyage. He sympathized with the Dutchmen, who suffered so intensely from the cold. He also sympathized with his fellow countrymen, who were working so hard. Under the circumstances he would be forced to leave the Arctic.

If the crew insisted, he said, he would return to Amsterdam, and the mission would be universally regarded as a failure. His own reputation would be at stake, and he would regretfully be forced to bring charges of mutiny against the crew.

The men knew what would happen to them if they appeared before an admiralty board established by the directors of the Dutch East India Company. The judges would be sea captains, and these ship's masters, regardless of nationality, regarded mutiny as the most heinous of crimes. Certain execution by hanging awaited every sailor on board if the *Half Moon* returned to Holland.

Hudson paused, then quietly informed the men there was an alternative. In fact, they could recover their self-esteem and good names. There was an excellent chance they could even win immortal glory.

Coming to the point of his speech quickly, he proposed that they seek a western sea passage to the Orient by way of the New World. Enlarging on his theme, he told them it was his personal conviction, after many years of intensive study, that such a passage existed.

The crew cheered enthusiastically.

Hudson put the idea to a vote, and the men supported him unanimously.

He had achieved his first goal, and knew there would be no rebellion when the men discovered they were sailing westward across the Atlantic.

But, apprehensive lest the superstitious seamen become unruly, which was always a possibility on any voyage of discovery, he told them still more about his plans, going farther to appease them than any other master afloat. There were two

possible routes, he said. One was by way of the Furious Overfall, which he himself had long preferred. The other, suggested to him by his friend, Captain John Smith, lay farther
to the south. Smith, he declared, was convinced that an open
waterway to the Pacific lay somewhere between the newly
established colony of Jamestown, in Virginia, and the mouth
of the St. Lawrence River.

The men agreed that they might enjoy greater success if
they followed the Furious Overfall, but Hudson cautiously
made no promises. As he well knew, the weather in the straits,
now named after Davis, that led to the Furious Overfall was
bitterly cold. And he had already seen how his crew behaved
in such a climate. Therefore, as was his prerogative, he reserved the right to make the final decision himself.

All hands raced up to the deck to change course. Wind,
snow, and ice were ignored, and even the Dutchmen who had
been longing for the tropics worked with cheerful vigor. In
spite of ice floes and dangerous currents, the *Half Moon* re-
versed herself in a remarkably short time and headed westward in the direction from which they had come. Harmony
was restored, and men of the two nationalities worked side by
side again.

The new era of amity had been established none too soon,
for on May 25 the *Half Moon* ran into the worst storm yet encountered on the voyage. Winds were so intense and seas
were so high that Hudson ordered Juet to remain with him on
the quarterdeck at all times. Thus the mate could take command quickly if the captain were incapacitated.

The lookout sighted the Lofoten Islands in the distance,
but had to come down from the crow's nest before being
blown overboard. Then the winds became so fierce that most
of the sail had to be taken in. Colman and John Hudson set

an example by risking their lives as they climbed high into the rigging to haul in canvas, and after some hesitation the men followed them.

But luck was with Henry Hudson now. The gale was driving him toward the west at a far faster speed than he could have maintained in fair weather under full sail. At four o'clock on the afternoon of May 28, he wrote in his log, the Faeroe Islands were sighted far ahead. The next morning the ship approached the islands, and the captain hoped to put into port for fresh water, bread, vegetables, and other food supplies. However, the seas were still very high, giant waves smashed over rocks outside harbor entrances, and whirlpools made navigation still more difficult. He prudently decided to sail on without putting into port at any of the nearer, smaller islands.

He realized, though, that it was imperative to keep the men in good spirits, so he ordered a small sea anchor cast overboard to act as a drag and slow the ship. His gamble succeeded, and on May 30 the weather became sufficiently calm for him to nose into the harbor of one of the larger islands in the rocky, volcanic chain that stood between Scotland and Iceland.

The natives were surly semibarbarians, a rough people who spoke the ancient tongue of their Norse ancestors. Usually they were peaceful, but on more than one occasion they had been known to swarm aboard a visiting ship and threaten to damage it unless they were given a ransom of cloth and firearms. So Henry Hudson took no chances, and anchored in the outerreaches of the harbor. He and Colman remained on board, and Juet led the crew ashore in two groups, using the captain's gig.

The inhabitants, shaggy men in sheepskin capes and sealskin boots, came down to the shore to watch the foreigners in silence, but no hand was raised against the intruders. The crew worked all day filling the casks with fresh spring water and carrying them out to the *Half Moon*. The task was arduous but uneventful, and was not completed until ten o'clock that night.

A bright sun rose in a cloudless sky the next morning, and spring was in the air for the first time since the departure from Amsterdam. Hudson buckled on his sword, jammed a brace of loaded pistols into his belt, and went ashore with the entire crew. He made signs to the natives that his intentions were friendly, and quietly made his way through the village.

Later he wrote in his journal, "The houses of the Faeroe Islanders are the strangest I have ever seen. They are tiny huts with roofs of grass. At this season the grass is new and still green. The houses are built so near to each other that we had to walk past them in single file."

Soon reaching the pasture lands and farms, the company spent several hours enjoying a brisk walk. After so many weeks at sea, the men were hungry for the feel of solid land beneath their feet. Occasionally the captain paused to inspect a small, bright flower or admire the view. But conditions were not ideal for a bucolic interlude. A large group of Faeroe Islanders armed with pitchforks and clubs followed the seamen at a distance, afraid the strangers intended to steal some sheep.

Returning to the village at noon, Hudson offered to barter for food. Colman went out to the *Half Moon* for trinkets stored in the hold, but the natives were contemptuous of beads, mirrors, and iron cooking pots. They raised so many sheep that wool blankets were of no interest to them, either. But at last they sparked to some knives that Hudson had concealed until the last moment. After long and exhausting dickering, he exchanged eight blades for a half-dozen sheep, slaughtered on the spot, two sacks of barley and another of a green, leafy vegetable which left a bitter aftertaste when the men later ate it raw as a "salat."

Then, satisfied with their purchases, the sailors returned to the *Half Moon*. They weighed anchor and set sail again, aided by a stiff breeze. For the next two weeks the weather remained fair, the wind was favorable, and no incident of note disturbed the tranquil day-to-day existence aboard ship. On June 15 the weather changed abruptly, and the *Half Moon* was assaulted by a violent storm that covered most of the Atlantic.

Again, for four days and nights, Hudson saw continuous duty on his quarterdeck. He lost his foremast, and gigantic waves smashed a portion of his bow, but he considered himself fortunate to have escaped with so little damage. The storm abated late on June 19, and the captain took advantage of the glassy calm that followed the storm to put his carpenters to work. They labored through the night, burning torches, and by dawn the repairs were completed. Hudson ordered everyone served double rations of food and tots of "brandywine" for breakfast, and at sunrise the westward voyage was resumed.

Hudson's log and Juet's diary for June 25 indicate that the seventeenth century was less civilized than anyone living in the age cared to admit.

A short time before noon, the lookout sighted a vessel moving eastward. Hudson immediately ordered all hands to their posts and, as a precautionary measure, directed that the small cannon be unlimbered. The guns were moved into place fore and aft, and by then the lookout was able to report that the ship was somewhat smaller than the *Half Moon*.

Hudson immediately ordered his crew to close with her.

The stranger tried to veer off, but the wind favored the *Half Moon*, which maneuvered nearer the approaching craft.

Then Hudson ordered his distinguishing pennant hoisted, and the Dutch flag was raised to the topgallants.

The other vessel did not respond, so Hudson also sent up an English pennant.

Still the stranger made no response.

Everyone on the *Half Moon* knew at once that she was neither Dutch nor English, and therefore could be considered fair game for plunder.

Henry Hudson may have known such freebooters as Drake and Hawkins, sea vultures who had made piracy respectable. Certainly he was a direct inheritor of their tradition. Under the loosely defined and even more loosely applied laws of the sea, it was no disgrace for the strong to attack the weak, provided, of course, that they were not of the same nationality. It was also considered unsporting and poor diplomacy to assault the ships of an ally.

As it happened, both England and Holland were at peace. The Dutch had recently concluded a treaty with Spain, obtaining a number of hard-won concessions, and England was at least technically not in a state of war with the Spaniards. Henry IV of France had built such a powerful army that no one wanted to fight him. His navy, however, was weak. And France was far away across the Atlantic.

Hudson continued to bear down on the stranger. "I desired," he wrote innocently in his log that evening, "to speak with her."

The smaller vessel had good reason to feel apprehensive about talking with strangers. She was now sufficiently close for Hudson to see a flurry of activity, but he could not make out the features of the men on her quarterdeck.

Then, belatedly, the little ship broke out her pennant. The excited lookout on the *Half Moon* did not know the Spanish ensign from the French, but was positive the craft was neither Dutch nor English. That was all Hudson needed to know, and he crowded on additional sail.

At that moment, however, the wind from the east died down, and a strong western breeze sprang up, aiding the stranger, which fled. Hudson had no intention of letting a prize slip from his grasp, however, and gave chase.

For six uninterrupted hours, from noon until early evening, the *Half Moon* relentlessly pursued her prey. Exploration was forgotten, the Furious Overfall faded into the dim recesses of Henry Hudson's mind, and neither he nor his crew cared about the glory of finding the western sea passage to the Orient. Booty in the hand was worth far more than immortality on the horizon. Her mission ignominiously discarded, the *Half Moon* sailed due east.

Her seamanship was superior to that of her intended victim. But the wind continued to favor the frightened stranger, and Hudson could not move close enough to fire his cannon. The gap between the two ships began to widen at about five in the afternoon, and it finally became evident that the odds were against the ungainly *Half Moon.*

Hudson and his men were deeply disappointed, but the chase was abandoned. The westward voyage was resumed, and Hudson sadly noted in his log that he had lost twelve hours of sailing time "through no fault of mine or lack of diligence in my men." That night the crew speculated fruitlessly on the identity of the plunder they had missed.

Four days later Hudson, navigating by the stars, believed that the so-called banks of Newfoundland were directly ahead. Soundings were taken, and the men cheered when they saw white sand and a variety of shells in the bucket that had been dropped to the bottom. They had reached the offshore waters of the New World.

But Hudson was not yet ready to plunge on toward his goal. Uncertain of what lay ahead, he wanted to add to his food stores. And, with the memory of his own earlier experiences in mind, he wanted to take home a cargo that would pay for the voyage, thus increasing his own wages. So he gave his mates instructions to search for fleets of fishing vessels, which were certain to be in these waters during the summer months.

On July 3, a bright, hot day, Colman had the watch when the lookout caught sight of a dozen ships at anchor to the southeast. The *Half Moon* approached the fleet boldly, and Hudson was undaunted when he saw the gold and white lily banners of France flying from the vessels' topgallants. It did not matter in the least that the ship he had chased might have been French and that her compatriots now outnumbered him by twelve to one. No one was afraid of fishermen, whose vessels were even slower and clumsier than the *Half Moon*. Also, no self-respecting master ever attacked fishing fleets. The potential prize was not worth the effort, particularly when there was wealth of the same kind to be taken direct from the sea. Therefore custom decreed that there be no fighting, no threats of force, in the waters off the Newfoundland coast.

The *Half Moon* and the French vessels exchanged polite greetings, and Hudson observed that large numbers of cod were being hauled aboard the craft. The supply, it appeared, was unlimited, even though the French had been active in these waters for almost seventy-five years. He ordered the *Half Moon* to inch closer, intending to try his own luck, but the commodore of the fleet sent him a curt signal.

"These waters are French," the message read, colored flags fluttering in the warm breeze.

The claim was absurd, and Hudson knew it, as did the French. But he was not inclined to waste time and effort arguing international law or taking a stand for principle. There were literally too many fish in the sea. So he decided to move farther south, where both cod and herring ran.

One of the Dutch sailors was an expert fisherman, and the captain relied on his judgment. Not until July 8 did they sail into an area that the seaman liked, and there they cast anchor. The man's wisdom was promptly and emphatically vindicated. In the scant space of five hours, 118 large cod were landed, and so many herring were netted that there literally was not enough salt on board to preserve the entire catch. That night the elated Dutchmen gorged themselves on fresh herring.

Hudson, however, incurred their displeasure by refusing to let them preserve any of the small fish. The salt supply being limited, he wanted to save it exclusively for cod, which commanded far higher prices in the European markets. The Dutch sailors grumbled as they continued to stuff themselves.

The next morning fishing was resumed, and again the cod catch was spectacular. By noon the last of the salt had been used. But the men continued to haul in herring for use in the next few days. The fish were kept alive by immersing filled nets in the sea and attaching them to lines that trailed behind the *Half Moon*.

Slowly the ship edged closer to the shores of North America, and at dawn on July 12 Hudson was called from his bunk by the officer of the watch. Directly ahead was an inviting, smooth beach with the whitest sand that any member of the company had ever seen. The captain ordered his ship maneu-

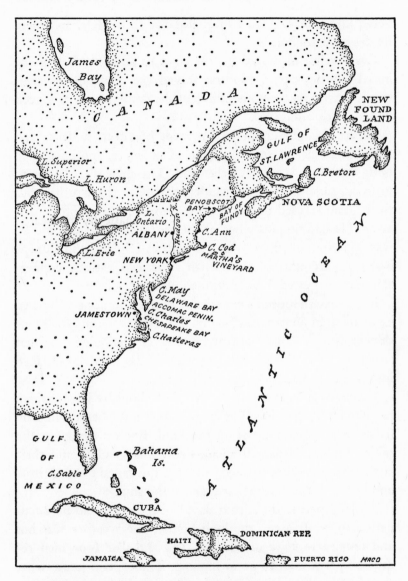

*Henry Hudson's third voyage, along the east coast
of North America.*

vered into a small cove a short distance to the left, and there he dropped anchor.

Every sailor clamored for the right to be a member of the initial landing party. Hudson solved the problem by arbitrarily giving the assignment to half the crew, which he placed under Juet's command.

Before the gig could be lowered, however, a dense fog rolled in suddenly, seemingly out of nowhere, and enveloped both the *Half Moon* and the land. The men were eager to proceed, regardless of the sudden change in the weather, but the captain refused to let them go ashore until the fog cleared away. He had no idea whether the area was inhabited, and he was apprehensive. Every literate man in England and Europe had read accounts of the North American natives, copper-skinned savages who were reputedly cannibals.

It had been Hudson's experience that a summer sun burned away mists in temperate climates. To his surprise the fog grew thicker as the day wore on, and a stand of thick pine trees that stood on a hill behind the sandy beach became transformed into a tantalizing, beckoning smudge.

He gave the men something to think about by having them prepare for an invasion. The cannon were unlimbered, and iron balls were brought up from the hold. But by sundown the sailors became impatient again. Land was so close and their anxiety to go ashore was so great that the captain had to issue another flat order confining them to the ship.

The fog persisted the next day, and the crew had no occupation to while away the long hours. The weather was hot and muggy in spite of the fog, and three or four men requested permission to go swimming. The captain knew what they had in mind. They were so close to the beach that if he allowed them to go into the water, nothing could prevent them from swimming ashore.

Rather than admit he was aware of their proposed trickery, he told them, with a straight face, that he felt certain the waters were shark-infested. The men promptly lost their desire for a swim.

The fog continued for several days, trying the patience of the entire crew. Henry Hudson was far more anxious than any of his men to go ashore. His explorer's curiosity was strained to the breaking point, and he needed all of his self-control to prevent himself from ordering the gig lowered and taking a landing party to the beach.

On July 17 the fog lifted for a short time, and the captain saw that he was anchored in an island cove near the entrance to a bay. In all, there were five islands lying offshore, and from Hudson's description of the area it seems likely that he stood near the northern lip of what later would be known as Penobscot Bay, Maine. He climbed up into the crow's nest himself, and with the aid of his glass saw a river emptying into the bay. This, in all probability, was the mighty Penobscot.

The mists gathered again as swiftly as they had dissipated. Hudson resisted temptation, once again ordering the entire company confined to the ship.

Later that morning his caution proved to be at least partly justified. Voices were heard off the port bow, and the men made out the sounds of paddles being dipped in the water. The entire crew was alerted, and the seamen ran off to get their blunderbusses and muskets. Hudson and his officers, armed with swords, moved to the rail to lead an assault on interlopers who might try to board the *Half Moon*.

Two dim shapes appeared in the fog, growing more distinct as they drew nearer. At last the men on deck made out two native canoes of birch bark, each occupied by three copper-skinned savages. The natives, their heads shaved on either side of scalplocks, were naked to the waist, and were clad only in loincloths of animal hide and moccasins decorated with seashells.

When the canoes drew alongside the *Half Moon*, Hudson saw that the savages carried no arms except crude knives made of stone. He rightly judged the natives to be harmless and allowed them to come on board his ship.

The Indians seemed unafraid of the heavily armed foreigners. Then the leader of the group addressed Hudson in halting but coherent French, bidding the company welcome. It was obvious that French traders or fishermen had visited the area and had established friendly relations with the savages. So Hudson relaxed.

He offered the Indians grilled herring, which they ate with relish. But they refused hardtack with such alacrity that he realized they were familiar with the tough biscuits. Their refusal did not surprise him, as most Englishmen and Europeans thought hardtack inedible, too. Only a man who had spent his life at sea actually enjoyed the taste of the thick, irregularly shaped chunks of double-baked bread.

Then Hudson had blankets, beads, and mirrors brought up to the deck, and the Indians calmly accepted these gifts as their due. The French, it appeared, had spoiled them.

In return for Hudson's hospitality, the leader of the savages told him there were large deposits of gold, silver, and copper nearby. Juet and a number of seamen became excited, but the captain himself remained skeptical. Men who had access to metal did not carry crude stone weapons, and he suspected that the Indian was lying. Perhaps, he reasoned later in his journal, previous visitors had made such insistent inquiries about gold, silver, and other precious metals that the Indian, wanting more gifts, compliantly told strangers what they wanted to hear.

The guess was shrewd—and accurate. Neither then nor later were any mines found in the area. And it became the habit of many Indian tribes living along the eastern seaboard of North America to tell similar bland, glib lies to several generations of settlers throughout the seventeenth century.

The Indians spent the better part of the day on board the ship, and when they departed they promised to see the visitors again. The leader indicated that, when he and his men came again, they would bring with them objects of great value for trading purposes.

The sailors imagined they would soon become wealthy, but Hudson sensibly discouraged their speculation. If the Indians owned anything worth trading, he said, the French would have made it their business to gain possession of these objects. He doubted whether the savages had ever seen diamonds, rubies, and sapphires, much less gold and silver.

The sky was clear at daybreak the next morning, and visibility was excellent in all directions. The fog had gone at last. The sailors thought they could go ashore now. But the captain had other ideas. He ordered the men to weigh anchor, and the *Half Moon* cautiously nosed into the bay, finally berthing near the mouth of the river.

Then, at last, the gig was lowered, and the master himself led the shore party. At approximately nine o'clock on the morning of July 18, 1609, Henry Hudson set foot on the soil of North America for the first time.

VI

Discovery!

Ɛ❧

TALL PINES AND TOWERING POPLARS, huge oaks and magnificent elms far larger and more stately than any to be seen in Europe, were everywhere. A hill stood a short distance from the river mouth, and Henry Hudson climbed it with his men to see the view. The sight of an impenetrable green mass, a sea of trees stretching out to meet the horizon, stunned him. For a long time he stood in awed silence, unable to speak or move.

"The wilderness of the New World," he wrote in his journal that night, "forms a vast natural cathedral. No work of man is its equal. Nowhere is there such natural grandeur. In many places the forest comes down to meet the sea, the green of leaves blending with the green water. I did not know whether to weep or cry aloud with joy, but in my heart of hearts I rejoiced to see the wonders wrought by God."

Henry Hudson had fallen in love with America at first sight.

When he recovered his equilibrium, he quickly remembered there was work to be done. Instead of leaving the preparation of a new foremast to his bo's'n, he personally selected the tree he wanted cut. Then, somewhat to the annoyance of the men, he hovered nearby while they trimmed and shaped it.

When the others returned to the *Half Moon* with Colman, the captain remained ashore alone, directing his second mate to supervise the mending of sails while Juet directed the emplacement of the new foremast.

There is no record of how Hudson spent the next few hours. Perhaps he returned to the hilltop to see the view again and meditate. It may be that he wandered through the silent "cathedral" of the forest wilderness.

Certainly the episode is significant. He had come to North America hoping to find an inland waterway that would take him to the Pacific Ocean and the Orient, but he had discovered a land that enchanted him. In view of the caution he had shown in refusing to permit the crew to go ashore during the foggy weather, it is interesting that he should have chosen to remain in the forest alone. Either he had lost his fear of the natives, or his delight with his surroundings made him impervious to that fear.

His only comment in his journal is laconic, revealing nothing. "Myself remaining on shore after the dispatch of the men to the ship, I signalled to the quarterdeck from the water's edge soon before sundown, and Juet sent my boat to fetch me and return me safely to the *Half Moon.*"

The following morning the entire crew made the trip ashore. Hudson had intended to refill the casks with river water, but one of the men found a natural spring. The water that bubbled out of it was so pure that even the unimaginative Juet noted in his diary, "It has as sweet a taste as brandywine."

Two of the Dutch seamen found a live lobster crawling near some rocks in shallow water, and soon the entire crew gathered to see the creature, which was much larger than the European crayfish with which some of the men were familiar. It seemed reasonable to assume that where there was one lobster there would be others, and the sailors spread out to hunt for them, splashing through knee-deep water, indifferent to the drenching spray of the surf.

In all, they caught thirty-one lobsters within a short time. As soon as the laborious task of transporting the filled water casks to the ship was completed, the whole company returned to the *Half Moon* for a feast.

In honor of the occasion, Hudson ate with his men. "The lobsters were boiled," he wrote in his log. "Their flesh is firm, and their taste more succulent than that of other shellfish."

The captain could do no right in the eyes of his first mate, and Juet made an observation in his diary, too. "Cap'n. Hudson," he wrote, "ate two lobsters. Colman and I ate one per each, as did the men. I saw them looking angrily at the Cap'n., and whilst they dared not speak their grievance, they were wondering why he should have eaten two when they were allowed only one per each."

Either Juet was mistaken about the number consumed, or someone's arithmetic was faulty. The company, including officers, numbered no more than twenty-one persons. Thirty-one lobsters had been caught. Therefore, even if Hudson had eaten two, there were enough left for others to eat a second, too, if they wished.

Hudson also wrote in his log, "I gave the men two jugs of wine from my private stores, and all were merry." If he, rather than Juet, is correct, the men enjoyed the occasion.

Soon after the company finished eating, the Indians who had canoed out of the fog to the *Half Moon* returned for a second visit. Apparently the savages hoped to receive more food and gifts. But when Hudson asked if they had brought him the promised information about the location of the gold, silver, and copper, they looked at him blankly. None, it seemed, could remember any previous mention of mineral wealth. Hudson was not surprised, but conveniently "forgot" to give them any more gifts.

The visit was unsuccessful in other ways, too. The Indians, displaying the natural curiosity of savages, edged toward the hatches and indicated by signs that they wanted to inspect the interior of the ship. The wine-flushed sailors immediately suspected that the Indians intended to steal their personal gear. Two Dutchmen and an Englishman quickly placed themselves in front of the hatch, drew their knives, and ordered the savages to leave. The Indians seemed somewhat bewildered by the sudden show of anger, but meekly went ashore again.

Early the next morning the officer of the watch gave an alarm. Scores of Indians were rowing out to the *Half Moon* in long canoes with blunted prows that resembled French longboats. Hudson immediately assumed that the savages were coming to repay the strangers for their gratuitous insults, and ordered all hands to arm themselves. The men dashed below for their blunderbusses, and the gun crews stood by their cannon.

To the astonishment of the entire crew, the Indians proved to be unarmed. The French-speaking leader stood up in the prow of a boat and called that he and his friends had brought furs to trade.

Hudson remained wary but allowed the natives to come on board his ship, a few at a time. The savages were as good as their word, and brought with them several bales of beaver and black fox. The captain knew little about furs but thought these specimens were excellent.

There were more surprises in store. The Indian leader announced that he would barter only for "red gowns." Neither Hudson nor any other member of the ship's company understood what the savage meant. An elderly Indian who was wearing such a garment came aboard from one of the boats. Hudson found it difficult to keep a straight face. The man was wearing a long nightshirt of red wool, an almost shapeless item of dress that was currently popular in England and Europe.

Luckily, Juet owned one such nightshirt, Colman had two, and several of the men owned one or more of these inexpensive oddities. Hudson took charge of the bargaining, and after a long afternoon the Indians finally departed. They carried off the nightshirts in triumph, leaving behind several expensive bales of fur that would command exorbitant prices in Amsterdam.

Hudson had not enjoyed the experience. "I felt like a merchant," he wrote contemptuously in his journal. It is ironic that he, whose name was subsequently given to the company that became the world's largest fur-trading concern, should not have been interested in the transaction. Apparently he failed to realize, too, that the furs of North America were worth more than all the gold and silver that other men eagerly sought. Like so many explorers, Hudson did not think in commercial terms. He had been pleased to salt codfish, which would earn him a paltry sum. But he could not grasp the significance of the prime beaver and fox pelts.

The crew had no chance to rejoice, either. The savages had left muddy footprints all over the *Half Moon,* and the captain ordered the decks washed and scrubbed before sundown.

On July 21 and 22 the sailors cut several spare masts, which they stored in the hold. There was no need for these extra masts, but Hudson apparently could not resist the opportunity to utilize magnificent trees in the way he knew best.

Then, on July 24, the men went out into the open sea in the gig, armed with nets and fishing lines. They returned with several large cod and a "holy butt," or halibut. As they had no more salt, they went ashore, intending to preserve the fish by smoking them over a fire. Apparently none of the men knew that smoking was a long and delicate process, in which foods required expert handling. One of the cod was burned to a crisp, so the attempt to preserve the others was abandoned. The fish were cooked and eaten on the spot.

At twilight some of the men were still on the beach, and the story of the sudden greed they displayed on this occasion is one of the most unsavory episodes in the history of the expedition. The camp of the fur-trading Indians was nearby, and several long, lightweight canoes were riding in the water. A group of the seamen, unable to curb their avarice, stole a boat and took it out to the *Half Moon.*

Then, not content with the mischief they had already done, they collected their firearms, went ashore again, and ran toward the animal-hide tents of the savages, brandishing their weapons. The Indians fled into the forest, and the sailors helped themselves to deerskin capes, moccasins, and other clothing. Then, laden with their spoils, they returned to the ship.

Henry Hudson unquestionably knew of these outrages committed by men under his command. But there is no record of whether he condoned their robberies, actually approved of their actions, or once again showed weakness when his men were determined to do as they pleased. Certainly he neither forced them to return the canoe and personal belongings nor punished them for their crimes. His log and journal are mute on the subject. Juet wrote about the incident in detail, and others confirmed the basic facts after returning to England.

Hudson's own position is suspect because of his subsequent behavior. Rather than return the stolen items, apologize, and make his peace with the Indians, he weighed anchor before five o'clock in the morning. By the time dawn broke, the *Half Moon* had put out to open sea, moving south under full sail. It is difficult to believe that, had he not shared in the guilt of the seamen, he would have fled.

Once at sea, he promptly forgot the matter and devoted his full attention to charting the coastline. Reducing sail, the *Half Moon* made her way slowly southward, and a few days later reached a wild, desolate and beautiful cape. Hudson thought he had found a hitherto unknown land and called his discovery, "New Holland."

But a closer examination of his maps convinced him that he was in error. "This," he wrote in his log, "is that headland which Captain Bartholomew Gosnold discovered in the year 1602, and called Cape Cod, because of the store of codfish that he found thereabout." He was right, and made new maps that added to the findings of Gosnold, another English adventurer-explorer.

Some of the men went ashore, returning to the ship with large bunches of wild, sweet grapes. The fact that fruit grew in the area was subsequently responsible for the mistaken impression of the Pilgrims and other early New England settlers that the region was a promised land, a land of milk and honey. The blazing heat of Cape Cod in midsummer also caused Hudson and his men to believe that the climate there was exceptionally mild. They had no way of knowing that New England winters were bitterly cold.

A small band of Indians was encountered, and several came on board the *Half Moon* for a brief visit. The savages smoked pipes with what the captain described as copper stems, and he was surprised to see that the tobacco they used was green.

In the following weeks the ship made her way slowly down the coast, sometimes moving out of sight of land, sometimes hugging the shore. In mid-August she stood off Virginia, but Hudson did not pay a visit to Jamestown, the colony established two years earlier by his friend Captain John Smith. Custom and national pride prevented him from dropping anchor there. Barring a grave emergency, no foreign ship would have been welcome in an English colony, even that of a Dutch ally commanded by an English master.

Somewhere off the coast of North Carolina, perhaps in the vicinity of Cape Hatteras, Hudson decided to turn northward again. He now proposed to search in earnest for the waterway that would carry him across North America and give him a sea passage to the Orient. Therefore, he knew, it would be necessary for him to make a close inspection of the entire coastline.

On August 19 the voyage north began. Two days later a storm was encountered, and some of the sails were ripped. But no serious damage was done. However, both Hudson and

Juet became apprehensive when the ship's cat, the only animal on board, ran from one end of the *Half Moon* to the other, howling. According to one of the most universally believed superstitions of the day, cats were capable of communicating directly with Satan.

But the omens of evil did not develop, although the ship was forced to fight offshore currents. Hudson briefly put in to bodies of water that later came to be known as Chesapeake Bay and Delaware Bay, but judged that neither of the rivers he saw was broad enough to open into sea passages to the Pacific. He hugged Cap May, still moving northward, and was so impatient to find his deep-water channel that he twice sent Juet to the crow's nest to search for it.

Early on the morning of September 2 the officer of the watch saw a brushfire burning behind some swamps. At daybreak the *Half Moon* glided past the gleaming beach of Sandy Hook, and soon afterward Hudson fulfilled one part of his great destiny. Arriving off the lower tip of what came to be known as Manhattan Island, he saw the mouth of the great river that bears his name.

Contrary to popular belief, Henry Hudson did not discover the Hudson River. Eighty-five years earlier, in 1524, Giovanni da Verrazzano, an Italian explorer in the employ of Francis I of France, reached the same spot and went ashore on Manhattan Island, where he and his men shot several birds and made friends with a band of Indians. A sudden storm forced him to put out to sea, however, and he had no chance to explore up the river itself.

Later in that same year a Portuguese master, Estevan Gomez, who was in the service of Spain, also arrived at the mouth of the Hudson River, which he named the St. Antonio. If he traveled up the river, he kept the information to himself. The news he brought back to Europe was so sparse that, like Verrazzano, his discovery created no stir.

Then, for the better part of a century, no other explorer appeared. Henry Hudson, bolder and more inquisitive than his predecessors, was more determined to find the sea passage to the East that they, too, had been seeking.

On the night of September 2 the *Half Moon* anchored somewhere in the vicinity of the Narrows. The next day was foggy, but the weather cleared around noon, and Hudson sailed close to Staten Island, anchoring a short distance offshore for the night. The next morning he sent his gig toward the land. He would have preferred to use the stolen Indian canoe for the purpose, but it had been rendered useless. It had been towed behind the *Half Moon*, and the current had driven it against the hull of the ship, crushing its prow. It floated on its side now, half-submerged. Hudson felt he had no alternative, and regretfully ordered the boat cut adrift.

The men in the gig returned, bringing with them several very swarthy Indians. The savages sang what appeared to be a chant of welcome. Juet noted in his diary that they were wearing bracelets of what seemed to be either gold or copper. Hudson wrote flatly in his journal that the jewelry was of copper.

On September 5 most of the crew went onto the mainland, led by the captain, to explore the forests of what was to become New Jersey. Once again Henry Hudson was enchanted by the North American wilderness. The oaks, he said in his journal, "are of a height and thickness seldom beheld." The linden trees caught his attention, too, and he declared, "They are of a beauty seldom beheld by men."

He was the first of the company to taste wild plums, a deep purple in color and incredibly sweet. There were red grapes and white in abundance, too, and vast patches of whortleberry vines. He thoughtfully ordered a hat filled with them for Juet, who had remained in charge of the guard on board the *Half Moon*.

Only one minor disturbance marred the visit ashore. A Dutch sailor made the mistake of walking through a growth of sturdy poison ivy. The others saw how his skin became blistered and swollen, studied the weed, and thereafter avoided it.

When the party returned to the ship, a dozen new visitors arrived. Two, who were treated with respect by the other warriors, wore headdresses made of brilliantly colored feathers set vertically in a band of deerskin. This type of headgear, which many people later came to identify, mistakenly, with all American Indians, so impressed Hudson that he obtained one in barter and took it back to Holland with him. So one of his lesser achievements is the popularization of the feathered Indian bonnet that has appeared in countless illustrations.

The Indians were otherwise modestly attired. Some wore trousers and shirts made of either elkskin or deerskin, worked until it was very soft and pliable. And, in spite of the heat, all sported capes of fox fur over their shoulders. Juet noted in his diary that their wrists flashed with yellow copper jewelry.

The natives indicated to Hudson through sign language that the river whose entrance he had glimpsed was very large. Here, he hoped, was the waterway to the Orient he had sought for so long. So, early on the morning of September 6, he sent Colman and four sailors in the gig to investigate.

The party rowed through the Narrows, finding the task so arduous that they raised a small sail. Colman was delighted with Manhattan Island, which was ablaze with yellow, red, and blue wildflowers. They went ashore, found large quantities of wild celery, which they tried and found good. Before they could return to the gig, however, a fog descended, forcing them to remain on the island.

The unsuspecting quintet sat patiently on some rocks, and were startled when two canoes appeared out of the gloom. Arrows whistled through the air, and one of the seamen died instantly with a shaft through his throat.

The other members of the party were at the mercy of the savages, too. But the Indians withdrew inexplicably, as suddenly as they had appeared. The fog became worse, and the group could not return to the *Half Moon* with the body of their dead comrade until morning. The seaman was buried that same day at a spot subsequently known as Colman's Point.

The stunning attack and death of the sailor confirmed the worst fears of the entire company. Hudson and his men had not trusted the Indians from the outset, and were convinced the savages were plotting to annihilate all of them.

The captain took immediate steps to protect the *Half Moon* and her crew. The gig was hauled up onto the main deck, and the ship was put into a state of siege. Exposed portholes were boarded up, the cannon were placed on deck ready for instant use, and the company was divided into two platoons, one under Juet and the other under Hudson himself. One unit slept and ate while the other stood duty on deck. Sentries paced the decks, a permanent lookout was stationed in the crow's nest, and the men carried firearms with them at all times.

Hudson placed one sensible restriction on the sailors. They were forbidden to fire a pistol or blunderbuss unless they received specific authorization from either the captain or first mate.

Virtually nothing was reported by either Hudson or Juet

about the funeral of the murdered seaman. Neither indicated in his notes whether a religious service was held or whether the man was buried very quickly, without a ceremony, so the escort could hurry back to the *Half Moon.*

After a day and night of great tension, the lookout gave an alarm early in the morning, soon after sunrise. A canoe filled with natives was approaching the ship! Fuses were lighted, and the gunners awaited a signal from the captain to fire the cannon.

Hudson stood on his quarterdeck, carefully inspecting the approaching craft through his glass. The savages appeared to be unarmed, but the contents of several large, bulky sacks made of woven reeds aroused his suspicions. He decided to hold his fire until he investigated.

The canoe pulled alongside, and Juet indicated, in pantomime, that he wanted to know what the sacks contained. The Indians opened one, and the men on the deck saw that it held grain of some sort. This was the introduction of Englishmen and Dutchmen to American corn.

The captain was not satisfied, and demanded that each of the other sacks be opened, too. The savages complied with the request, and Hudson decided to take a chance when he saw that all contained grain. He permitted the Indians to come on board, one at a time, and forced each to submit to a personal search for concealed weapons before being allowed to go to the poop deck.

At last the crew, accompanied by the visitors, went aft. There a dramatic confrontation awaited the Indians. The four survivors of the Manhattan expedition appeared, coming up onto the deck through a hatch. Then a tarpaulin that had concealed the gig was removed. Captain and crew searched the faces of the savages to see if the Indians showed any sign of recognizing either the survivors or their boat.

The expressions of the wooden-faced Indians did not change.

"Had they indicated by a cunning light in their eyes that they had knowledge of the foul murder," Hudson wrote in his journal, "I was prepared to order my company to exterminate all without delay."

The trick having proved unsuccessful, bartering was begun. Hudson had little interest in trading, however, and concluded a deal quickly. Several strings of beads and two mirrors were traded for the bags of corn. Then the visitors were unceremoniously hustled off the ship, and the state of siege was resumed.

Another tense night passed. Soon after breakfast the following morning the lookout called a sharp warning. Two "great longboats," as Hudson called them in his log, were approaching. There were at least a score of husky warriors in each. All were armed, some carrying bows and arrows, others holding spears with tips of either copper or stone.

The captain immediately made up his mind to take no chances. He let the war canoes draw nearer, then walked to the rail of the main deck and fired a pistol. A half-dozen gulls sunning on a nearby rock flew into the air. But the birds were no more frightened than the savages. One canoe pulled away and started back toward the shore. Before the paddlers in the other could recover their wits, however, the captain drew his second pistol from his belt and pointed it at the natives.

Then he summoned Juet, who indicated in lively pantomime that two savages were to come on board as hostages. There was a murmur of dissent in the war canoe, but the Indians were too frightened to disobey the command. And when several sailors went to the rail and aimed their cumbersome blunderbusses at the natives' boat, all signs of opposition vanished.

A line was thrown overboard, and two of the warriors meekly climbed up to the deck. The canoe was then driven off, the seamen cursing and threatening to shoot.

Scarcely more civilized than the Indians, the sailors treated the two hostages abominably. The savages were forced to wear ludicrous combinations of clothing and parade up and down the deck while the crew laughed and taunted them. Hudson made no attempt to calm his men. Like them, he could not forget that a member of his company had been murdered.

That night Hudson reached a major decision. The hostages' continued presence on board made further attacks unlikely. Therefore he could explore the great river in relative safety. Soon, if all went well, he would know whether the waterway opened onto the Pacific Ocean.

At daybreak the order to weigh anchor was given, and the *Half Moon* sailed slowly through the Narrows. Hudson wrote in his journal that this was one of the great moments of his life. He spent the better part of the day cruising in New York harbor and saw so many thousands of gulls on what was later to become Ellis Island that he called it Gull Island in his charts.

Then, having mapped the harbor to his satisfaction, he gave the command to sail up the river, and at dusk he anchored in the vicinity of what would become Forty-Second Street. An epic voyage of exploration was under way.

VII

The Great River—and Beyond

ಕಾ

HENRY HUDSON made a slow, almost leisurely journey up the river that was to bear his name. He hoped he had found his sea passage to the East, but knew that, even if the waterway failed to take him to salt water, he had discovered a major stream well worth investigating in detail. Therefore he made careful charts, taking frequent soundings, testing the speed of the current, searching for underwater rocks, sandbars, and other obstructions. Whenever he found whirlpools or other phenomena he inspected them in detail. And at the same time he wrote in his log long reports of the surrounding countryside.

A sixth sense apparently told him he had discovered a virgin land of great potential value. He wrote about the trees he saw and other foliage. He described the terrain on either side of the river bank. And even when he did not go ashore he studied the soil through his glass and made notations to the best of his ability, indicating whether he found sand, clay, or loam.

On September 13 he anchored the *Half Moon* near the spot where, about three hundred years later, Grant's Tomb would be erected to house the remains of the great Civil War general who later became President of the United States. There he was treated to another of the New World's many delights. Four canoes manned by Indians paddled out to the ship, and when it was ascertained that the savages were unarmed, they were permitted to approach. In each of the craft were several large woven baskets filled to the brim with fresh oysters, which the natives wanted to trade. Hudson was agreeable and gave the Indians more beads and a few mirrors in exchange for the delicacies. The company feasted on oysters early in the afternoon. Then the anchor was weighed, and the *Half Moon* moved upstream to the vicinity of what came to be called Spuyten Duyvil, where she stayed for the night.

The next day Hudson sailed almost as far as present-day West Point. He remained on his quarterdeck the entire time, making detailed notes, and was fascinated by the high bluffs that would come to be known as the Palisades. "Nature was in one of her happier moods when she created these cliffs," he wrote in his log. "They stretch for approximately fifteen miles on the west bank of the river, and are ever a delight to the eye. Behind this natural wall stretches the great forest, which lies like a cloak over most of the New World. The river flows swiftly, and many birds circle and soar overhead. I have recognized the osprey and the heron, larger than their like in England, and others whose names I do not know. These latter may be birds known only to the continent wherein we now journey."

He observed rugged hills, some of them large enough to

be called mountains, and also mapped the valleys, most of them on the east bank. One somber thought was also recorded in his journal: "I doubt not that there is much game to be found in the forest. On cliff ledges I have seen the nests of birds, and would like the taste of fresh eggs on my palate. But, it having been proved to our sorrow that the natives hereabouts are bloodthirsty, I dare not send a landing party ashore for fear that more of my men will be foully and wantonly murdered."

On September 15 the explorers lost their insurance against Indian attacks. The two hostages, who were being held in a small cabin that was bolted from the outside, managed to pry away the boards that covered the cabin's porthole. They wriggled through, jumped into the river and swam ashore before their absence was detected. In fact, the crew learned of the escape only when the pair had reached the eastern bank and stood on shore, shouting insults, before disappearing into the woods. For a short time Hudson considered sending off a pursuit party, but wisely refrained. The savages were completely at home in the wilderness, which he had already learned to treat with respect. It was far better, he decided, to continue his voyage without running more risks than necessary.

The captain was impressed by two sites, those on which the towns of Kingston and Peekskill were later built, and drew freehand sketches of the waterfronts at both places. "Boats could find adequate shelter at these places in foul weather," he wrote, "and at both it would be not too great a chore to build houses and forts that would obtain commanding views of the surrounding land. Sentries at these forts could prevent surprise attacks if the forest were well cut back and brush cleared away."

All that week new parties of Indians continued to paddle out to the *Half Moon,* sometimes in small numbers, sometimes in large groups. These savages were friendlier than those encountered in New York harbor. They frequently laughed, they were voluble, and their manner contained no hint of guile. Hudson gradually became less apprehensive, and by September 18 was sufficiently at ease to accept a dinner invitation from a local chief. Juet went, too, and in his diary referred to the Indian as "a governor of this country."

The captain described the occasion in one of the longest, most cheerful entries in his journal: "I sailed to the shore in one of their boats, which was made of white bark, well gummed at the seams with the juices of another kind of tree. My host was an old man, who was the head of a community which consisted of forty men, seventeen women, and children so numerous as they ran from one place to another that I could not count them.

"These I saw dwelling together in one large house well constructed of oak bark, and circular in shape, so that it had the appearance of being well and truly built, with an arched roof. In the center of the roof was a hole, and on the ground beneath it a pit lined with stones, that was used to cook meals in inclement weather. At this time, the weather being fine, meals were prepared in another pit near the house.

"This house contained a great quantity of maize, which looks and tastes not like the maize our farmers grow. When eaten fresh, it has a sweet taste, which does not disappear even when pure salt is crumbled onto it. When older and preserved, it resembles our own grains. But even when powdered it loses not its yellow coloring, and the taste remains sweet, a fact at which Juet and I marvelled.

"The house also contained fine beans of last year's growth,

and there lay near the house for the purpose of drying, enough to load three ships, besides what was growing in the fields. These are an industrious people, who do like to fill their bellies and preserve the produce of their fields. The women labor over the crops, and boys also. But men hunt for game in the forest and take fish from the river, there being great schools of white-fleshed fish therein that are fine-grained and pleasant to the taste.

"On our coming into the house, two mats were spread out to sit upon. Immediately, some food was spread, served in well-made red wooden bowls. This food was a paste, gray-brown in color, with a distinctive odor that I could not recognize. I was loathe to eat it, but the old man ate from his bowl, dipping in his fingers and letting the substance cling to them. So great was his hospitality and so jovial his manner that I was sensible to his feelings and did eat, too. The food had a taste both familiar and strange, and when I made inquiry, the old man showed me it was a pulp taken from the inner rind of trees, which was mashed and mixed with whortleberries. He who has never tasted the rind of trees would not welcome it as a dish to be savored, but I recommend it to all. I know not the name of the tree from which it was taken, this tree being strange to me, but I will know it again when I see it. The leaves thereof are long and slender, tapering at the ends, and the tree, like all trees of the New World, stands very high in the forest.

"Two men were despatched at once in quest of game, who soon after brought in a pair of pigeons they had shot with bows and arrows. The skill of the Indians with these weapons is very great. It pleases me that the people of this nation are my friends, and my resolution to stand firm against those nations of Indians who are my enemies is doubled.

"They likewise killed a fat dog, and killed it in great haste with shells they had got out of the water. Then they roasted it, and when it was cooked they cut pieces of meat from the carcass with shell knives and ate it with their fingers. In my own land dogs are members of a man's household, and are not eaten. But I was again sensible to the feelings of my host, and cut myself a portion with my knife, Juet doing likewise. The taste was not sickening, as I had feared, and had I not seen the dog killed, would have thought I was eating freshly roasted pork.

"The Indians supposed that I would remain with them for the night. But I could not abandon my men to the elements, nor my ship to the mercies of savages who might be otherwise than good-humored, and after the dinner was done made ready to return to my ship.

"The natives are a very good people, for when they saw I would not remain, they supposed that I was afraid of their bows, and taking their arrows, they broke them in pieces, and threw them into the fire.

"The skill of these natives with their weapons filled Juet and me with wonder. Their knives are made of shells taken from the fresh water of the river. It being known that fresh-water shells are not as hardy as salt-water shells, I could scarce believe what I saw when I watched how deftly they used these tools. Their bows and arrows are fashioned with these same crude knives, and their arrow-heads are fashioned of chipped stones, yet their aim is as true as that of a marksman who has mastered the art of shooting a pistol. Their axes are fashioned of stone also, but the natives cut down trees with almost as little effort as does a man who carries an ax of steel.

"I gave them a gift of knives before I took my leave of them, although Juet was fearful that these weapons might be turned against us. But I had already judged the character of the old man and his people, and know we had nought to fear from them. Their gratitude at receiving such knives, on which we ourselves place so little value, gave me the greatest satisfaction I have known since I began my voyage up the river.

"The land is the finest for cultivation that I ever in my life set foot upon, and it also abounds in trees of every kind and description. Were our own industrious farmers to settle here, they would soon transform this wilderness into a Paradise where no man need ever go hungry. And there are in the forests deer, wild boar, and other game in such numbers that no table need ever lack meat. For variety there are fish in hordes to be taken from the river, and multitudes of plump birds overhead, all good for the eating thereof. Never have I beheld such a rich and pleasant land."

Whether Hudson, writing enthusiastically in his cabin after his visit ashore, realized that his description of the Hudson River valley would have an electrifying effect on millions of poverty-stricken men and women in England and Europe is a matter of conjecture. It seems likely that he was indeed thinking in terms of colonization when he hinted that farmers from the other side of the Atlantic could tap the vast resources of the New World and develop them.

If so, he stands almost alone among explorers of his own and previous ages. Even the practical, hardheaded John Smith devoted pages of his reports to glowing accounts of gold and silver that, allegedly, the lucky settler might locate. Only Sir Walter Raleigh, like Hudson, seemed to understand that North America promised her future settlers riches of a far different sort.

Yet, strangely, Hudson recognized neither the potential of the fur trade nor of the lumber industry. Literally as well as

figuratively, he stood so close to the forest that he failed to
see the worth of the trees.

What concerned the explorer most, after his pleasant interlude on shore, was the growing suspicion that the river was
not the waterway to the Orient that he was seeking. The
channel was growing narrower, and the old chief had indicated
to him that there was no body of salt water ahead.

On September 19 the *Half Moon* anchored in the harbor of
present-day Albany, and the next morning the captain sent his
Dutch bo's'n and four other men farther upstream in the gig.
They returned at dusk with crushing news. The river became still narrower, they said, and the bed became increasingly
shallow.

Hudson's hopes flickered, but did not die. Other channels
became narrow and then widened again. Magellan had persisted, and the famous Strait that bore his name had taken the
Spaniards into the waters of the south Pacific, much to their
own astonishment. There was a possibility, even though it
was only remote now, that the river might open onto the sea
approaches to the Orient.

The crew was ordered to make ready to resume the voyage
on the morning of September 21, but before the anchor could
be hoisted, a group of natives appeared from the interior. They
came from a large Indian town they called Schenectadea, and
Hudson was able to make out by their use of sign language
that the name meant, "A place that one finds when one
marches through the woods of tall pine."

Something in the attitude of these savages made the captain
and his company fearful, though they could not define the
precise cause of their apprehension. Hudson therefore invited
the chief and two others, apparently senior warriors, to his
private quarters, where he offered them unlimited quantities

of potent brandywine. His intention, as he wrote in his journal, was to "try whether they had any treachery in them."

The Indians had never before tasted liquor, and of course drank too much. At first they became jolly under its influence, laughing, then singing, cavorting, and dancing. An Indian woman who was a member of the party did not join in the revelry, however. She sat quietly, drinking nothing, with her head bowed and her hands folded in her lap. Juet, who had so little good to say of anyone, praised her for modesty when he described the occasion in his diary.

Unfortunately, the old chief drank so much that he fell unconscious. The other Indians were afraid that the strangers had put their leader under a magic spell, and hastily carried him ashore to remove him from the baleful influence. When he failed to recover within a short time, a delegation returned and presented Hudson with strips of leather to which shells had been sewn. He recognized these as the savages' equivalent of money from the way they handled the leather, and accepted two or three out of curiosity. Later the Dutch East India Company would make identical currency, which was then given to its officials who traveled to the New World. Thus Hudson, unwittingly, became a party to the counterfeiting of "wampum," which most North American Indian tribes used.

While the savages were hurrying back and forth between the shore and the *Half Moon*, the captain had an opportunity to ponder the plans he had made, and decided to change them. It might be too dangerous, he decided, to take a large ship up a narrow, shallow stretch of river. If the *Half Moon* suffered serious damage, he and his company could be stranded on a continent of barbarians, thousands of miles from home.

So, instead, he sent his carpenters to cut down a tree and

fashion a larger mast for the gig. They worked through most of the day and part of the night. The next morning the bo's'n and the four men who had gone with him previously started upstream again, aided by a sail that enabled them to double their traveling time.

The incident involving the old chief was not yet closed, however. He awakened, after a long, deep sleep, feeling fit again. His comrades rejoiced, and returned to the *Half Moon* to express their thanks. They also brought Hudson more wampum, two different kinds of smoking tobacco, and, most welcome of all, a dressed side of venison. The meat was roasted immediately, and the sailors forgot their restlessness as they smelled the cooking meat.

After dinner a chilly rain began to fall, reminding the company that summer was drawing to a close and that colder weather was coming. The bo's'n and his party returned well after sundown with flatly discouraging news. The river became so narrow and shallow, they said, that a ship the size of the *Half Moon* could not navigate in her waters. The captain therefore decided to proceed no farther, and the return voyage began early on the morning of September 23, aided by a stiff breeze from the northwest.

The wind was so strong, in fact, that the ship was driven onto a mud bank and was stranded there until afternoon, when the rising of the tide in the ocean far to the south floated her free. Hudson thought it remarkable that the tides should be felt so far inland, a phenomenon that occurred on few other rivers.

The first few days of the voyage downstream were pleasant. When the *Half Moon* was mired in still another mud bank, the men went ashore for chestnuts, which they subsequently roasted. The captain's mind seemed to be turning more and more to thoughts of colonization. The trees that lined the river, he wrote in his journal, would make sturdy house walls. The wood would be useful in everything from shipbuilding to fashioning casks. Large, flat stones that resembled slate, he also declared, would be the best material he knew for roofing.

When a very strong south wind forced the *Half Moon* to anchor again, the old Indian chief who had been intoxicated paid the ship another visit, escorted by two large canoes filled with warriors and, apparently, the members of his own family. He introduced two elderly native women to Hudson, and two very shy young girls. The captain accepted gifts of food and tobacco, and in return gave the savages several steel knives, which they appreciated greatly, and some blankets of heavy wool, at which the women gaped in wonder. One of the elderly squaws forgot her lifelong training and burst into tears, no longer caring that the custom of her people demanded impassivity in the presence of strangers.

Hudson offered his visitors no liquor, and later wrote in his journal, "The Red Indians of the New World cannot drink spirits with equanimity. Many Europeans can drink spirits for whole days at a time without feeling ill effects, but these primitive people become crazed after they drink only a small amount." He was the first to notice this inability of the Indians to tolerate liquor. Thousands of incidents through the next centuries of settlement were to prove his observation correct.

The natives whose hospitality the captain and his first mate had enjoyed on their voyage upstream came to see them again. The chief begged Hudson to return to his lodge for another meal, but the wind was favorable, and the offer was refused, the master thinking it wiser to continue his journey whenever the weather permitted.

The season was changing rapidly, he knew, and shifting

winds constantly reminded him of the desirability of reaching the open sea at his first opportunity. South winds, which made progress downstream difficult, alternated with breezes from the northwest, so the *Half Moon* was anchored whenever she headed into a stiff wind.

"It is better," Hudson said in his log, "that we lose a few hours at anchor than be driven once again onto mud flats."

Juet and several sailors went fishing in the gig one day when the ship rode at anchor, and enjoyed excellent luck. "We caught so many mullets, basses, and barbits," the mate declared in his diary, "that our nets were filled to overflowing."

Below present-day Poughkeepsie another band of Indians appeared, bringing on board the skins of some small animals they hoped to trade. Hudson was not impressed by the pelts, but gave the savages some beads and mirrors in return for them. Ironically, his description of the skins indicates they may have been mink, later to become one of the most expensive and highly prized of furs.

The difference in the attitudes of Hudson and Juet is emphasized by entries in their records on September 30. The mountains, Juet said in his diary, "look as if some metal or mineral is in them." But Hudson was more interested in the site of what would become Newburgh, and said in his journal that it was "a very pleasant place to build a town on."

The following day, not far from present-day Peekskill, trouble erupted. Still another band of Indians came on board to trade animal pelts. While the bargaining was in progress, one warrior remained in a long canoe, paddling near the stern. Thinking the strangers too busily occupied to notice him, he climbed up onto the rudder of the *Half Moon*, crawled through the porthole of the cabin occupied by Juet and Colman, and stole a pillow, two shirts, and two swords. He was seen as he crawled back into his canoe. The Dutch bo's'n immediately fired a blunderbuss at him, hitting him in the chest and killing him instantly.

The other Indians were alarmed by the power of the strangers' weapons and fled. Some jumped overboard and began to swim toward the shore. Others climbed into canoes and swiftly cut the lines that held the boats fast to the *Half Moon*. The gig was riding in the water, and Juet led a party to it, expertly sliding down a line. The mate's one desire was to recapture his stolen property, for other Indians had climbed into the canoe with the dead man and were paddling for dear life as they made for the shore.

One warrior, who was swimming within arm's length of the gig, reached out a hand and tried to tip it over. Presumably the savage thought it as easy to upset this heavy boat of oak as it was to capsize a lightweight canoe of bark.

The ship's cook, who had been preparing dinner at the time of the theft, was a member of the gig's party, and still held his meat cleaver in his hand. With one swift blow he cut through the savage's forearm, and the Indian was drowned.

The canoe loaded with the stolen property was abandoned at the river bank, and Juet managed to recover his belongings before heading back to the ship. Hudson, afraid that the Indians might try to counterattack in force, weighed anchor at once, crowding on sail. He went as far south as possible, and did not halt for the night until long after sundown.

A heavy guard was maintained now, and the next morning, just as the *Half Moon* was about to resume her voyage, another large party of Indians paddled out from the shore. Hudson studied them through his glass and recognized one of the braves who had been made captive and had suffered humiliation at the hands of the crew before escaping.

While half the ship's company worked to weigh anchor and hoist the sails, the other half, under Juet's command, stood ready to repel boarders. The Indians requested permission to come onto the *Half Moon*, but were refused. A shower of arrows whined around the heads of the sailors, several lodging in the sails. Juet promptly gave the order to fire, and two or three of the braves were killed.

The warriors became panicky and headed back toward the shore. Hudson ordered the crew to sail south at maximum speed. Then he noted that, a short distance ahead, more than one hundred warriors were gathered on a point of land that jutted far out into the river. The combination of current and wind made it impossible to swing a vessel the size of the *Half Moon* toward the far bank in time to avoid another rain of arrows.

Hudson acted decisively. Without changing his course, he ordered Juet to fire the smaller of the ship's cannon point-blank into the throng. The gun roared, and as nearly as Hudson could judge from the quarterdeck, at least two of the savages were killed. Most of the others, frightened by the deep, resonant bark of the weapon, fled into the forest.

Nine or ten of the Indians, however, demonstrated fanatical heroism. Quickly leaping into a long war canoe, they paddled with all their might in an attempt to overtake the ship. Their mission was suicidal, as they soon discovered. The small cannon was quickly moved from the bow of the *Half Moon* to the stern. Juet himself aimed it, while the sailors lining the deck steadied their cumbersome blunderbusses on the rail. Then the sailors waited until their foes drew near.

At short range, it was almost impossible for the firearms to miss their targets. The cannonball made a gaping hole amidships, sinking the canoe and killing one of the warriors. Three or four others, according to the accounts of both the captain and first mate, died of musket shots. The rest, presumably, were drowned.

The *Half Moon* sailed on, and soon the silence of the wilderness encompassed the ship again. All immediate danger was now averted.

Hudson wanted to leave this hostile countryside as rapidly as he could, and did not anchor for the night until he drew near the site of what later became Hoboken, on the western bank, opposite the lower portion of Manhattan Island.

In spite of the day's tensions, plus the distinct possibility that the savages might attack again, Juet now had other matters on his mind. The color of the cliffs on the western bank fascinated him, and one in particular seemed so promising that he made a sketch of its location. It was a white-green, "as though it were either a copper or silver mine," he wrote in his diary. "I think it to be one of them, as the trees that grow upon it are small, whilst all others nearby are very large." No minerals of value have ever been found beneath the earth's surface there, it might be noted.

Hudson was more concerned with possible trouble, and wasted no effort speculating on potential mineral wealth. He posted a strong guard, and himself remained on duty all night, pacing up and down the quarterdeck in order to keep awake. In spite of his apprehensions, the night passed quietly. But the *Half Moon* and her crew were not yet safe. A heavy fog rolled in from the sea at dawn, making it impossible to see as far as the prow from the quarterdeck.

The captain realized he had to remain at anchor all day. He posted another guard, with Juet in charge, and went to bed. Less than an hour later he was summoned from his bunk because unexpected difficulties had arisen. Tides and currents were so tricky that the anchor was drifting across the bottom. The *Half Moon* had to move still farther downstream and anchor again, a hazardous maneuver in the thick mist.

There she remained for the better part of twenty-four hours, her master and crew expecting an Indian assault at any moment. Then, almost magically, the weather cleared and a favorable wind sprang up, seemingly out of nowhere. Hudson noted in his log that he set "main-sail, sprit sail and top-sails, and steered away east-south-east, and south-east by east off into the main sea."

The rich, promising—and menacing—land that he had explored lay behind him now, and a major adventure had come to an end.

But a great decision still had to be made. The chief purpose of the voyage had not yet been fulfilled. The Furious Overfall had not yet been investigated, and a sea route to the Orient had not yet been found. The northwest passage was still elusive, still undiscovered.

Neither Hudson nor any member of his company suspected that the land they had explored and mapped would become the principal seat of wealth and commercial power in the Western Hemisphere, dwarfing the fortunes of the Orient.

All the captain knew was that he had not yet accomplished his mission. He was tempted to spend the winter in New foundland so that he would not have far to sail in his search for the Furious Overfall when spring came. Before making up his mind, he sounded out Juet. The first mate was evasive, and refused to express a forthright opinion.

So the captain called in his Dutch bo's'n, who enthusiastically supported the idea of staying in the New World through the cold weather. But Hudson wanted to take no chances with a rough crew that might mutiny, and he asked the bo's'n to make seemingly casual inquiries.

The results of the poll were far from encouraging. The men were sick of unsalted fish. Their supplies of beef were gone. There was very little herring left. If necessary, they knew, they could eat the salted cod stored in the hold. But the prospect of a cod diet, supplemented by other fish that might be caught through the winter, definitely did not appeal to them. Without exception the men wanted to return to civilization.

"In my heart I could not blame them," Hudson wrote in his journal. "No man is courageous on an empty stomach. The last of our ale was long since drunk, and there were no spirits on board except the last cask of brandywine from my own store."

Nevertheless, he was reluctant to abandon the venture that meant so much to him. So he thought of a compromise that, he hoped, would win the approval of the crew. Summoning the company to a meeting, he proposed that the *Half Moon* sail to Ireland. There, he said, he could obtain meat and spirits, and there would be less distance to sail in the spring. The men unanimously agreed.

What caused Hudson to alter his plans while crossing the Atlantic is not known. Perhaps the more troublesome members of the crew changed their mind and demanded that he bring the voyage to an end. There is a hint, but only a hint, that he encountered trouble on the high seas. His first letter to the directors of the Dutch East India Company after his return to civilization requested that seven sailors whom he considered "lacking in efficiency" be replaced.

Whatever the incidents that took place at sea, the voyage was swift. On November 7, slightly more than a month after

leaving New York, the *Half Moon* dropped anchor in the
harbor of Dartmouth, in Devonshire, England.

Henry Hudson's third voyage of discovery, which was to
bear fruit beyond the wildest dreams of any man then alive,
had come to a sudden and abrupt end.

VIII

The English Tempest

ह**

IT WAS HENRY HUDSON'S INTENTION when he landed at Dartmouth to spend the winter there. He was so anxious to resume his voyage at the first possible moment that he made no immediate plans to visit his family in London. For that matter, he wrote no letter to his wife telling her of his safe return to England until two full weeks had passed. His sole desire was to refit the *Half Moon*, obtain needed supplies and replacements for his crew, and make ready for another voyage.

On November 8, less than twenty-four hours after he landed, a packet ship putting out to sea with mail for the European continent carried a long communication he had prepared for the directors of the Dutch East India Company.

In it he outlined, with almost maddening brevity, his accomplishments. Then, filled with enthusiasm, he proposed that he sail again in early spring. This time he wanted direct authority to hunt for the northwest passage. He felt positive, he told the Dutchmen, that such a passage to the Orient existed.

He would be happy to sail again on the same contractual terms he had accepted for his third voyage. His own wages, it seemed, were of only secondary importance. Far more pressing was the need for supplies, ammunition, trinkets for natives, and repairs that would enable the *Half Moon* to reach her goal. She was not a perfect ship, he admitted, but he had become accustomed to her peculiarities, and believed that if the appropriate repairs were made, he could take her anywhere on the earth's seas.

In all, he told the directors, he needed the staggering sum of fifteen hundred florins in Dutch gold, a fortune by any standard. He made it very plain, too, that seven members of the crew had to be replaced.

The schedule Hudson proposed was remarkably precise. He would leave Dartmouth at the beginning of March and would reach the waters of the New World by the end of that month. He planned to spend the month of April and the first half of May fishing off the coast of Newfoundland. As he intended to carry a large supply of salt, he declared, he would return with enough cod, halibut, and other fish to finance the entire expedition. In mid-May, when the weather grew warm enough, he would begin his explorations, which would occupy him until mid-September. Then he would return to Holland by way of Scotland, explaining that he believed his fish catch would bring higher prices from the Scots than from any other people.

The letter dispatched, Hudson went to work putting his log, maps, and charts into final shape for his employers. This task occupied all of his time, and he continued to live on board the *Half Moon.* The sailors slept on the ship, too, but had nothing to do beyond keeping order, which took very little time. Consequently they spent most of their days and evenings in the taverns and inns that lined the waterfront of Dartmouth.

Hudson had ordered his men to tell no one where they had been or what they had seen on the voyage. He believed, correctly, that the directors in Amsterdam should be the first to learn the details of what had transpired on the expedition.

Unfortunately, however, he expected too much. The sailors, warmed by liquor, the fires in taprooms, and appreciative audiences, could not keep their mouths shut. They boasted of having found a great, broad river that swept through incredibly fertile countryside. They spoke of mammoth trees, edible game, and rich fur pelts. They described waters teeming with fish. Then, embroidering on their tales, they hinted at gold and silver in the interior, and gems scattered on the floors of mountain caves.

The innkeepers listened avidly, and so did the masters of small ships, traveling merchants, and a scattering of lawyers and other professional men who had business in Devonshire. Gradually rumors drifted back to London. Each day fresh stories reached the capital, and each day they became more exaggerated.

At last the accounts, in which fact and fancy were now freely mixed, reached Whitehall, where King James I met daily with the members of his Privy Council. England was still riding on the crest of an exuberant wave of nationalism that had reached new heights during the reign of the late Queen Elizabeth I.

The dour, complicated James of England and Scotland was a man of many faults, but a lack of intelligence was not one of them. He was shocked that one of his subjects should have made major discoveries which would benefit a foreign nation.

It did not matter in the least that Henry Hudson had been following an international custom in force for more than a century and a quarter. The captain had done nothing wrong. In fact, England herself had benefited from the discoveries of the Cabots, who had been hired foreigners.

Nevertheless, the more King James thought about the matter, the angrier he became. And when the King was outraged, the Privy Councilors lost their tempers, too. Something drastic had to be done at once, James said. His advisers unanimously agreed.

In the meantime, Hudson continued to work on his maps and charts, unaware of the growing tempest in London. He did not know, either, that the ship carrying his initial letter to Amsterdam had been crippled by a storm at sea and forced to put into an English port for repairs. As a result of the delay, the letter did not reach the directors of the Dutch East India Company until the last days of December.

Hudson's maps, charts, and log were dispatched to Holland in December, too, and actually may have reached their destination before the first letter arrived. The captain also made excerpts from his journal for the edification of the men who had financed his voyage. These fragments, carefully preserved in the files of the Dutch East India Company, survived through the ages, and are all that remain of the journal. The original, fuller and more detailed, may have perished with Hudson himself. Scholars have conducted diligent searches for the valuable document through the centuries, but have never been able to locate it.

In mid-December, 1609, however, Henry Hudson felt he had good reason to be proud of himself. He had discovered a major river on the North American continent, and knew his report would arouse interest in many nations. He had completed the arduous, painstaking task of writing his reports and making accurate maps. And he saw no reason why the Dutch would refuse to send him on another voyage. The future appeared bright.

He made plans, at long last, to spend Christmas with his wife, children, and grandchildren in London. His men were anxious to obtain leaves of absence, too, so he paid them their wages to date, granted them the right to spend the next four weeks where they pleased, and instructed them to return to Dartmouth in January. Most of the Englishmen indicated that they would accompany him on the journey to London. A few of the Dutch sailors said they would stay in Dartmouth, but the majority planned to cross the North Sea for visits to relatives in Holland.

Hudson, Juet, and several others hired horses and started out for London. The captain was in a lighthearted mood, and hoped to enjoy his holiday. "He entertained us on the road with stories," Juet sourly remarks in his diary, "but his humor left much to be desired." Then, suddenly, only a few hours after the party left Dartmouth, the unexpected blow fell, stunning them.

A high-ranking officer of King James' own household regiment, accompanied by a squad of heavily armed troops, met them on the road. Hudson was handed a parchment document signed by two of the King's ministers and bearing the impressive seal of the Privy Council. An official Order in Council had been issued, directed against Henry Hudson, captain and master, and all English members of his company.

The Order severely chastised the explorer for his participation in a venture "to the detriment of his own country." He and all English members of his crew were forbidden to leave England again without first obtaining the express permission and approval of the Crown.

The officer and troops then escorted the adventurers to London. James and his advisers were taking no chances, and wanted to make certain that Hudson and his men did not slip across the North Sea to Holland. "We were treated," Juet declared with understandable bitterness in his diary, "like murderers or other criminals of the most despicable sort. From the moment we encountered the King's men, we were held under close arrest."

Hudson had cause to feel deeply apprehensive about his future. The wording of the Order in Council hinted that he might be brought to trial on charges of treason. The fact that he had merely followed long-established custom in accepting employment from the Dutch after the English-owned Muscovy Company had refused to support another venture into the unknown might be discounted.

Hudson must have thought a great deal about Sir Walter Raleigh on the long ride to London. Raleigh, who had held the rank of Admiral in the Royal Navy, had been one of England's most distinguished sons, a famous explorer and fighting man who had been a favorite of Queen Elizabeth's. In spite of his renown and high position at court, he had been arrested on charges of conspiring against the Crown, and his trial in 1603 had been a mockery of justice. Sir Edward Coke, his judge and chief prosecutor, had treated the Admiral with brutal disdain and found him guilty on flimsy evidence. Raleigh still languished in the Tower of London, and it was common knowledge that King James intended to have him executed as soon as public sympathy for him died down.

If a man of Raleigh's standing and popularity could be

treated with such disdain, and his services to his country so lightly forgotten, someone like Henry Hudson appeared doomed. It would matter little that the new whaling industry, which was making so many Englishmen wealthy, owed its beginnings to Hudson. He had no prominent sponsors, no mighty lords who would be willing to defend him. And his greatest exploits, on his third and most recent voyage, had been made under the Dutch flag. The case against him was clear, according to James' standards, if the Crown intended to prosecute.

Instead of returning to London in triumph, Hudson went home in disgrace, surrounded by pikemen who wore the King's uniform. A guard was posted outside his house, and although he was not arrested, soldiers accompanied him whenever he went out, even on the most trivial errand. The constant attendance of the soldiers depressed him, and he stayed at home, refusing to accompany his wife to church on Christmas morning. It was only a matter of time, he believed, before he would be hauled off to prison. His sole hope now was that he had acquired sufficient fame to be lodged in a Tower suite, like Sir Walter. The alternative was to be cast into a commoners' prison, where living conditions were so deplorable that men often died of disease or starvation before their frequently postponed cases were brought to trial.

News of the Order in Council did not reach Amsterdam until sometime in January, after the directors of the Dutch East India Company had finally received Hudson's first letter, together with the documents he had mailed them later. They requested him to come to Amsterdam immediately to discuss future plans. Rather than write a reply, he copied the Order in Council in his own hand and sent it to them.

The brusque, unfair treatment accorded Hudson by his own

monarch created a stir in Holland. The directors of the Dutch
East India Company became very angry, and their government
directed the Dutch minister in London to protest. Van
Meteran, the ranking Dutch official in London, went to
Whitehall late in January and made an impassioned speech to
King James. Citing precedent for the hiring of Captain Hud-
son, he declared that friendly relations between the two
nations were being arbitrarily endangered.

James, who was in one of his less verbose moods that day,
made only a few remarks in return. He enjoyed the friendship
of the Dutch, he said, and continued to respect them. He
wished them well in the further exploration and settlement of
the territory that Hudson had explored and that now, consequently, became a Dutch possession. However, he said flatly,
the Order in Council spoke for itself.

There appeared to be little or nothing the Dutch could do
to help Henry Hudson. But people in England were sympa-
thizing with him, and expressed their opinions freely. The
fierce English love of justice and freedom asserted itself. Common men made Hudson's cause their own. Nobles who held
unflattering views of the King openly declared that Hudson
was being punished for a crime he had not committed. Others
demanded that he be brought to trial so the case against him
could be disproved. Sir Walter Raleigh's friends, who could
do nothing to help him, now became Hudson's champions.

Then the financiers of England began to stir. Dining together at inns and private homes, they reviewed Hudson's
past. He had proved to their satisfaction that it was not possible to find a Polar or northeastern route to the Orient by sea.
But he continued to maintain that he knew of a northwest
passage. Even if he failed to find it, they argued, he might
discover another fertile land similar to the great river valley

that was located "somewhere to the north of Virginia," as several described it in letters to each other. Gradually a new idea took shape. Nothing in the Order in Council prevented Hudson from sailing to the New World again—under English auspices.

One of the first to recognize the potential benefit to England of such a voyage was Sir Thomas Smith, the most influential merchant in London. A founder of the English East India Company, he was passionately committed to the belief that a nation—and her citizens—became wealthy through international trade. Only a few months earlier he had launched the largest merchant ship in the world, *Trade's Increase*, which he had financed out of his own pocket. Sir Thomas, an extraordinary man in any age, was convinced that trade could not be expanded without discovery and exploration. Therefore he was holding a school for sea captains at his own house, where experts delivered lectures on navigation, geography, and other subjects.

Sir Thomas sat down with two of his good friends to discuss the situation. One of them was Sir Dudley Digges, a young gentleman who was a member of a powerful family, an Oxford graduate who had long been an admirer of Henry Hudson and his exploits. In fact, Digges had written and published at his own expense a handsomely bound and illustrated book on the northwest Passage after Hudson's return from his second voyage. The third member of the triumvirate was John Wolstenholme, later knighted, a Yorkshire landowner who had a keen interest in discovery.

The three decided to pay a visit to Hudson. They found him in an exceptionally depressed state of mind, as he had just learned that a Dutch naval officer, Commander Laurens Reael, was being sent to Dartmouth to sail the *Half Moon* back to

Amsterdam. Hudson considered himself permanently disgraced.

But he quickly forgot his problems when Sir Thomas asked him a single question: would he like to sail again, under the English flag and with adequate English financing, to seek the northwest passage?

"Captain Hudson's pleasure was so great," Wolstenholme wrote to his wife, "that he leaped out of his chair with joy, sending it crashing to the floor."

With Hudson's enthusiastic assent assured, Sir Thomas and his colleagues had only one more hurdle to overcome. It was a major obstacle, to be sure—the surly opposition of King James, who never forgave those who, in his warped opinion, had offended him.

The trio chose wisely, and paid a call on Henry, Prince of Wales, the King's eldest son, at the private room he maintained for his many business transactions at Number 17 Fleet Street. Henry, who literally killed himself by overeating before he could succeed his father on the throne, was one of the most remarkable young men in England. A patron of the arts, an enthusiastic devotee of discovery and exploration, he was also a student of astronomy and other sciences. He was, too, a patriot with a sharp eye for talent that would enhance England's glory and power. What was more, he had great courage, and had stanchly supported Sir Walter Raleigh throughout the Admiral's trial. "Only my father," he is supposed to have said contemptuously, "would hold such a bird in such a cage."

Prince Henry readily agreed to receive Henry Hudson in a private audience.

The following day Hudson, accompanied by Sir Thomas and his other new friends, went to Fleet Street, trailed by the ever present troops. The commander of the guard detail was deeply embarrassed when he discovered the party's destination, and discreetly retired with his men so the Prince of Wales would not see them if he happened to glance out through his leaded windowpanes into the street below.

Hudson, who was awed by no man, seemed at home with the Prince from the start. Henry asked scores of questions, showing that he possessed a sound working knowledge of geography and navigation. He was also familiar with the major outlines of the voyage in the *Half Moon*, and pressed Hudson for details. The captain answered readily, holding back nothing.

Finally, in a burst of candor, he told Prince Henry and the three gentlemen his secret. He wanted to find Davys' Furious Overfall, which he felt certain would give him a sea passage to the East.

That was the final touch, and Henry needed to hear no more. He promised to speak to his father at once, and said he would have word the following day. But even the Prince of Wales had to wait his turn at Whitehall when the King was in one of his withdrawn moods, and forty-eight hours passed before James consented to listen to his son.

They spoke privately, behind closed doors, and there is no record of what was said. But the results of the conversation were made known immediately. The Prince emerged in triumph to announce that the close surveillance of Captain Hudson was being ended by royal decree, and the captain would sail on a new voyage in an English ship, manned by Englishmen, carrying an English commission.

The King's reasons for changing his mind are obvious. James, who was no fool, realized he had gone too far. Himself a patriot, he wanted to utilize the abilities of a great explorer to his nation's benefit. He did not feel as deeply antagonistic to Hudson as he did to Sir Walter, and therefore was willing to take a graceful way out of his dilemma. It would have been embarrassing had wealthy proponents of trade like Sir Thomas Smith lost their respect for the Crown.

Hudson and his sponsors went to work immediately. It was now early March, and the captain wanted to sail for the New World at the first possible moment. A new company was formed, with Sir Thomas as its chairman. Prince Henry, Sir Dudley, and Wolstenholme were its directors. With the Prince of Wales himself as one of its sponsors, only formalities had to be observed to obtain a patent from the Lord Privy Seal. Sir Thomas, like Hudson, was not a man to wait idly, and began an energetic search for an appropriate ship. Meanwhile Hudson began to hire a carefully selected crew.

Sir Thomas soon learned that the bark made famous by Captain Weymouth's explorations, the *Discovery*, was available. She was broad-beamed, an excellent sailor, and had an exceptionally stout hull that would protect her against ice floes. Furthermore, she needed only minor repairs. The directors of the new company bought her, with Hudson's enthusiastic approval. In the meantime, so many investors wanted to buy shares in the corporation that Sir Thomas was besieged at home, at inns, and in the streets.

Hudson, too, was inundated by requests from sailors and would-be adventurers who wanted to join him. He had his choice of England's finest seamen, and it is astonishing that events proved him to be such a poor judge of character.

A great deal is known about most members of the *Discovery*'s crew. The first man hired was Robert Juet, the first mate. Whether Hudson was still unaware of Juet's personal antagonism to him or continued to overlook the man's opinions because of his excellence as an officer is not known. Why

Juet elected to sail again with someone he despised is equally mysterious. Perhaps he was hungry for more glory, or it may be that he was attracted by high wages. Sir Thomas and his associates opened their purse strings, and Hudson was paying his men more than any other master.

Three other seamen had been members of Hudson's crew on one or more of his voyages of exploration. Philip Staffe, the carpenter, was an industrious, competent workman, close-mouthed but reliable. Arnold Lodlo, a product of London's slums, was able to fill any position on board ship. Michael Perse, who held an able-bodied seaman's rating, was a rough giant capable of absorbing all the punishment that gales and cold weather could inflict on him.

John King, the quartermaster, was known to the captain as an honest man, an essential quality in the person who would deal with the ship's stores. It was later found that he had an unpleasant disposition and a hot temper. Francis Clemens, the bo's'n, was forty years old, perhaps the oldest of the sailors. He had first gone to sea as a boy, and felt more at home on a heaving deck than he did on land. There was no question of his competence.

In the light of his previous experiences, Hudson decided he needed a ship's physician and hired an eager young surgeon from Portsmouth, Edward Wilson, who was twenty-two years old. He was a gentleman who had never before gone to sea, and viewed the voyage as an adventure. So did Thomas Woodhouse, an Oxford undergraduate who was a student of mathematics. He had been recommended by Sir Dudley, which made it necessary for Hudson to accept him. As this was Woodhouse's first voyage, too, he needed training. Because of his background, the captain hoped to use him as relief for the helmsman.

Sylvanus Bond, the cooper, had spent all of adult life before the mast, and seemed very quiet, almost gentle. Adrian Motter, of Middlesex, who held an able-bodied seaman's rating, carried letters of recommendation from previous masters he had served. It did not occur to Hudson that these letters were forgeries, which had been made for Motter by a clever, dishonest penman. Nicholas Syms, an able-bodied seaman, was silent and withdrawn. William Wilson, another who held the same rating, would not have been hired by a master who had studied character. He was foul-mouthed, always cursing, bragged about his exploits with women and his capacity for drink, and actually quarreled with some members of the crew before the voyage began. Several other able-bodied seamen are only names to posterity. They include Michael Butt, Syracke Fanning, John Williams, Adam Moore, and John Thomas.

Bennett Mathues, the ship's cook, had once served briefly in the employ of Lady Smith. Sir Thomas vouched for the man's ability as a cook. Nothing was said, apparently, about his erratic temperament. Abacuk Prickett, who was carried on the manifest as an apprentice seaman, was one of the most complicated of the crew. He had worked in London as a haberdasher and then had become Sir Dudley's valet. His manner was suave, and he made it his business to be pleasant, agreeable, and when dealing with his superiors, ingratiating. Neither Sir Dudley nor Hudson suspected that he was ambitious, a ruthless schemer who hated the wealthy, the powerful, and the renowned.

One member of the expedition actually spent only one day on board the *Discovery*. This man, whose name was Coleburne, had been hired by the sponsors of the voyage to act as personal adviser to the captain. He had served with Weymouth, and there is reason to believe he caused that distinguished explorer a great deal of trouble. In Coleburne's case, Hudson was able to take his man's measure very quickly and act accordingly. While the bark was still moving down the Thames from London to the open sea, Coleburne was forcibly placed in a small boat and compelled to row ashore. He carried a sealed letter from Hudson to the investors. Presumably this communication explained why the captain had chosen to take such drastic action. Coleburne may or may not have delivered the letter, the contents of which were never made public.

Even greater mystery surrounds the engagement of one other member of the crew, Henry Greene, the son of a gentleman farmer from Kent. Soon after Hudson's return to London from Dartmouth, Greene appeared at his door, armed with various letters of introduction. His purpose in calling, he explained, was to express his admiration for a man who was, it must be remembered, in disgrace at the time.

Hudson appreciated the gesture so much that Greene soon became a member of his household, and lived with the Hudson family until the *Discovery* sailed on her fateful voyage. In spite of the captain's preoccupation with his own problems during these months, he could not have failed to learn something of his protégé's habits, all of which were bad.

Greene, a handsome young man with a glib tongue, had "the broad shoulders of a river bargeman, and even greater strength," according to Juet's graphic description in his diary. Greene associated almost exclusively with harlots, procurers, and gamblers, much to the dismay of Katherine Hudson, who complained that her house was becoming a headquarters for London's worst riffraff. Greene could pick a man's pocket with the ease of a professional criminal, and Katherine suspected that he and a bawd who was his constant companion were members of a counterfeiting ring. Her fears were at least partly realized when, shortly before the *Discovery* sailed, the woman was arrested for passing counterfeit coins.

But Greene could do no wrong in Henry Hudson's eyes. The young man had come to him publicly and had shaken his hand at a time when most Englishmen had believed that the master of the *Half Moon* was a traitor. Greene asked that he be allowed to accompany the expedition. Hudson not only agreed, but wrote a letter to the young man's mother in Kent, urging that she advance her son the considerable sum of five guineas to buy appropriate clothes for the voyage. In this communication Hudson painted a glowing picture of his protégé's future. When they returned to England, he said, he intended to use his influence to obtain a place for Greene in Prince Henry's personal guard of honor. He had already broached the subject to the Prince, he declared, and had every reason to believe that Henry would agree.

Mrs. Greene, who had been afraid her son would end his days on Tyburn Hill, where criminals were executed before large, bloodthirsty crowds, must have breathed a deep sigh of relief. Through a miracle, her son had found a famous patron. She sent the five guineas, and the new wardrobe was purchased from a tailor named Venson. This worthy, who knew Greene by reputation, insisted upon being paid in advance.

It is significant that Greene's name did not appear on the ship's manifest. Nor was he present with the rest of the crew when the owners came on board for a ceremonial inspection and a farewell cup of sack with the master shortly before sailing. In fact, he did not join the company until the *Discovery* reached Gravesand, near the mouth of the Thames, where he rowed himself out to the ship in a small boat.

Perhaps Hudson had spoken to Prince Henry on Greene's behalf, as the letter to Mrs. Greene stated. But it appears that the master of the *Discovery* did not want worldly men like Sir Thomas and Sir Dudley, who knew the gossip of London, to learn that he was taking a man with such a disreputable name and background on the voyage. Hudson actually went to a great deal of trouble to enable Greene to join him. Inasmuch as the captain had never been much of a conniver, and Greene subsequently demonstrated that scheming and double-dealing were basic to his nature, it seems probable that the latter was responsible for the elaborate and deceitful plan.

The last name on the manifest was that of John Hudson, who was listed as a cabin boy. Syms was also originally designated as a boy, but his rank was later changed to that of seaman. Young Hudson, who had been called a mate on the *Half Moon* without performing the duties of an officer, did not serve as a cabin boy on the *Discovery*. His status was never more nor less than that of the captain's son, and although he climbed into the rigging with the others and shared all of their hazardous duties, he was never accepted by the sailors as a full-fledged member of the crew. Life before the mast must have been very difficult for John on all four voyages, as his father, not wanting to show favoritism, rarely invited him to a meal in the master's quarters.

The preparations for the voyage were frantic but orderly. Sir Thomas' money and influence made it easy for Hudson and John King, his quartermaster, to buy the supplies they needed. Thanks to the quiet intervention of Prince Henry, construction work on a new warship was halted at yards in Southwark, across the Thames from London, so the *Discovery* could be made ready for sea in time. Everything Henry Hudson wanted was granted quickly and without fuss. He learned how useful it was to know the right people, in the right places.

His own status changed literally overnight. Instead of being shunned by courtiers and other gentry, his company was now eagerly sought. Men who could not get Sir Thomas' ear made overtures to the captain in the hopes of being allowed to invest money in his enterprise. One noble, whose initials were F. L., sent an expensive shawl of embroidered lace to Katherine Hudson, along with a note hinting that the donor would appreciate a word in the right quarters that would enable him to participate financially in the voyage.

Hudson accepted his new standing gracefully, and if he felt at all cynical, he kept his private opinions to himself. He reappeared at the inns where he had often dined in past years, but otherwise did not change any of his habits. He was too busy preparing for his expedition to spend time with sycophants who smiled or frowned in imitation of the King.

In mid-April all was ready, and Prince Henry accompanied Hudson to a public audience at Whitehall. King James wished the explorer well and urged him to win fresh glory for England. Neither the monarch nor his subject mentioned the previous winter's unpleasantness. The entire interview lasted no more than a quarter of an hour, and a squad of Prince Henry's guard escorted Hudson home. As soldiers had dogged his footsteps before his restoration to favor, he may not have appreciated the gesture.

A heavy rain fell through most of the day on April 16, but the sky cleared late in the afternoon. Hudson sent his son to notify the other members of the crew that they would leave on the noon tide the next day.

Soon after dawn on April 17 the captain and his company took Communion at the Church of St. Ethelburga, in Bishopsgate, where a similar ceremony had been held just prior to

Hudson's first voyage. The guests who assembled for this occasion indicated how high he had risen in the esteem of his countrymen. Archdeacon Richard Hakluyt, who rarely made public appearances, was on hand. Prince Henry appeared with his retinue of officers and other gentlemen. Sir Thomas was present, of course, with his entire family, and Sir Dudley, who had overslept, arrived before the benediction.

Katherine Hudson, resigned to her husband's incessant travels, sat with her sons. She showed emotion only when John came up to her after the service. Then, for a moment or two, she wept, but gained control of herself. A captain's wife was required to display courage in the presence of the families of crew members, even though she was also a mother bidding farewell to her son.

The entire party repaired to the *Discovery*, which was anchored at St. Katherine's Pool in the Thames. It could not have been accidental that the mooring was directly below the windows of Sir Walter Raleigh's prison suite in the Tower. Londoners, sensitive to such gestures, saw Prince Henry's hand in the delicate but nonetheless definite slight to the King.

Members of the crew went on board at once to make ready for the sailing, and Juet took charge on the quarterdeck while Hudson showed the Prince of Wales, Sir Thomas, and the other distinguished owners through the ship. The sailors were permitted to go ashore again for a few moments to say a last farewell to their relatives.

In the captain's quarters, toasts were made by the Prince and Sir Thomas. Both spoke briefly, aware that time was important. Hudson's reply was equally short. Then the party went ashore, and the captain said good-bye to his wife, children, and grandchildren. Moving down the wharf again, he paused for a few earnest words with Hakluyt. Both men gestured emphatically, emphasizing their words. By this time the entire crew had assembled on the *Discovery*, and stood at sailing stations, awaiting the captain's pleasure.

But Hudson apparently forgot the tide as he warmed to his discussion with Hakluyt. Eventually it became necessary for Juet to have a gong sounded. Tides would not wait, even for noted geographers and famous explorers. Hudson and the Archdeacon exchanged bows, and the captain sprinted to his quarterdeck.

There his manner became more dignified as he gave the order to weigh anchor and cast off. The crowd on the dock cheered as the *Discovery*'s sails were hoisted. Then the bark began to move, slowly at first. She gained speed as she swept downstream, small craft scurrying out of her path.

When the ship arrived off Whitehall, a few minutes' run from her anchorage, Hudson ordered the English flag hoisted as a gesture of respect for the King. As it happened, James was otherwise occupied at the time, and did not see the *Discovery* pass down the river. Presumably someone later told him of the courtesy.

The last to leave the wharf were Prince Henry and Sir Thomas, who walked together, arm in arm. Both felt confident that the expedition they had financed and supported would make history. Neither they—nor anyone else, for that matter—had the faintest idea of what lay ahead for the master of the *Discovery* and his crew.

Only Archdeacon Hakluyt entertained serious doubts about the existence of a sea passage to the East. He was becoming more conservative as he grew older, and at a somewhat later date wrote that he warned Hudson, in their final conversation, not to expect too much of the Furious Overfall. "It would be a boon to all mankind if there were such a passage," Hakluyt wrote. "But Nature is seldom that kind."

Henry Hudson did not share his friend's reservations. On the contrary, he felt completely optimistic as he set out on his fourth and last voyage, the greatest adventure of his life.

IX

Secrets of the Furious Overfall

ॐ

HENRY HUDSON wanted to reach the New World as soon as possible. It had been his intention to leave on the *Half Moon* early in March, and now, on board the *Discovery*, he was six weeks behind schedule. He hoped to make up part of the lost time by increasing his sailing speed, even though he was moving against the prevailing winds, which blew from the west. He still wanted to spend several weeks fishing for cod in order to pay for the voyage, an idea that had appealed to the hardheaded Sir Thomas Smith. If necessary, however, he was prepared to cut down the weeks of fishing, as discovery and exploration were far more important than mere moneymaking.

The captain drove his crew hard, and the *Discovery* flew westward. On May 5 she stood off the Orkney Islands, on May 8 the lookout sighted the Faeroes and on the eleventh the ship approached the coast of Iceland. Then, suddenly,

Hudson's luck changed. Heavy fog and contrary winds made it impossible to continue the voyage.

Reacting with the resignation of a seaman who knew that cursing would not improve the weather, Hudson put in at an inlet on the western shore of Iceland. Here previous visitors had found hot springs that made it possible to bathe in the open, no matter how cold the winds.

For the next two weeks the company spent most days ashore. The men hunted and fished, went for long walks, and amused themselves by taking daily baths in the hot springs, a luxury rarely enjoyed by sailors who never bathed when at sea.

The springs were heated by the fires that burned in Iceland's active volcano, Mt. Hekla. The demons inside the mountain awoke from a long sleep during the *Discovery*'s stay in the inlet, much to the distress of Prickett and several other members of the crew. Smoke poured skyward, and at night sparks could be seen shooting up into the air above the lip of the open crater. While others were content to shoot partridges, ducks, geese, and a half score of other wildfowl, which they roasted every night, Prickett was afraid that the entire crew would suffer a fate similar to that of the birds if the volcano erupted.

Hudson, ever curious, wanted to climb the mountain and look down into the crater. But when he suggested the idea to the men, Prickett became so hysterical that he abandoned the scheme. It was far better to maintain the crew's spirits than to give in to the master's natural desire to investigate everything he deemed worth exploring.

Then, for the first time on the voyage, Henry Greene caused a disturbance. One morning, with nothing better to occupy him, he deliberately teased young Wilson, the surgeon, who finally lost his temper and gave Greene a tongue-lashing. The quarrel took place on board ship during the captain's absence on shore, and Greene took full advantage of his opportunity. He promptly invited Wilson to accompany him to the beach, where they would settle the matter with their fists.

A surgeon was regarded as an officer, and fighting between sailors and officers was contrary to the code of the sea. But the outraged Wilson either knew no better or did not care, and accepted the challenge. The two men battered each other for half an hour or more. Greene won the fight, in part because he was stronger, in part because he had taken part in countless London street brawls and therefore had gained valuable experience.

Hudson happened to come down the beach just as the fight ended. Naturally he asked what had happened, and a half-dozen witnesses began to talk simultaneously, giving him contradictory versions of the affair. The captain should have upbraided both men, but made one of the greatest mistakes of his life by supporting Greene. In the weeks since leaving London he had found that Wilson could be very caustic. Now, without pausing to weigh his words or think of the possible consequences, he remarked to Clemens, the bo's'n, "Wilson has a tongue that would wrong his best friend."

Then, suddenly remembering his position, he sternly ordered both participants to return to the ship, saying he would deal with them separately there. But Wilson had overheard the comment to the bo's'n, and was so insulted that he refused to go back out to the *Discovery*. It became necessary for the captain to take the surgeon aside and talk to him at some length before Wilson finally agreed to continue the voyage.

That might have been the end of the unfortunate incident,

as Hudson had the good sense to punish Greene by withhold-
ing his allotment of ale and other spirits for a full week. But
Robert Juet made the matter infinitely more complicated. The
mate had been alone in his cabin, drinking, when the quarrel
had taken place. As he had been in temporary command during the master's absence, it had been his responsibility to halt
the argument and prevent the fistfight. Feeling guilty because
he had been derelict in his duty, Juet, who was still under the
influence of liquor, deliberately made trouble.

He told several of the men that Greene was a spy in the
captain's private employ. "When we go home," he said, "he
will crack the credit of anyone who won't bow down to him."

The second in command of the expedition presumably was
privy to the captain's secrets. Many of the men accepted Juet's
statement as the literal truth. Thereafter a gulf separated Hudson and his crew, and it became increasingly difficult for both
sides to build a durable bridge over the chasm. The seeds of
discord sown by the mate would create a tragic and bitter
harvest.

The captain did not learn of his immediate subordinate's
astonishing—and untruthful—remarks until the *Discovery* had
resumed her voyage. When several members of the company
came to Hudson separately, and hesitantly, to repeat the comment, he was stunned. Unable to accept their word, he summoned Juet and asked him point-blank if he had made the
statement. The mate tried to evade, but Hudson persisted. At
last Juet confessed, but his attitude was defiant rather than
penitent.

An urgent, immediate problem confronted Henry Hudson.
He wanted to sail back to Iceland, put Juet off the ship, and
let the disloyal mate arrange for his own transportation back
to England when the next fishing fleet put into Iceland's

harbors. The best way to deal with such a vicious and irresponsible officer would be to get rid of him at once. However, there was no one in the company capable of taking his place. Neither the quartermaster nor the bo's'n, the two principal noncommissioned officers, was qualified to act as the master's deputy, relieve him on the quarterdeck, and take over acting command when he ate and slept. If Juet were left behind at Iceland, the *Discovery* would be unable to continue her voyage.

Hudson finally came to the reluctant conclusion that if he gave in to his feelings, he would be compelled to return to England for a new mate. At the very earliest, barring mishaps and bad weather, he would not reach his present position in the Atlantic again until mid-July. By then the summer would be too far advanced for him to follow the Furious Overfall to the Orient—or wherever it might lead him.

Pulled in two directions, he vacillated for forty-eight hours. Finally his yearning for discovery overcame his emotions and his common sense. Rather than admit temporary defeat, turn back, and sail again the following spring with a mate and crew of unquestioned loyalty and devotion, he made up his mind to push ahead.

Juet knew that the captain had been pondering his fate. When he learned that the *Discovery* would press on toward Greenland, he realized he had won a great personal victory. His vanity was so great and his opinion of the master so low that he immediately jumped to the conclusion that Hudson was afraid of him. He was wrong, but did not know it, and in his ignorance became an even more dangerous foe.

Hudson's decision made, he now concentrated on his great task. He probably knew as much as any man alive, perhaps more, about the area into which the bark was now sailing,

Greenland, the waters beyond it, and the portion of the North American continent that lay far ahead. Portuguese navigators had sailed to the American mainland in the last quarter of the sixteenth century, and both Hakluyt and Prince Henry owned copies of their crude maps. Undoubtedly Hudson had seen and studied these charts. One, drawn around 1580, actually contained a vague and distorted version of what later came to be known as Hudson Bay.

As recently as 1602, Captain Weymouth had reached Davys' Furious Overfall. But his crew had been so frightened by huge, erratically whirling ice floes that he had been compelled to turn back. All of George Weymouth's papers, including his log, were locked in Hudson's desk. Gifts from Plancius, they were among his most precious possessions. He also owned copies, made for him by Hondius, of some remarkable early fifteenth-century papers. A Norwegian seaman variously known as Bartsen, Barty, and Boty had written a detailed description of Greenland and its surrounding waters for the edification of his fellow Norse adventurers.

The island was settled, Hudson knew, by a people descended from early Scandinavian explorers and northern Indians. Some lived in houses of stone; others spent their winters in dwellings made of ice blocks and their summers in tents of animal hides. Their religion was a strange blend of Christianity and barbaric paganism. They raised sheep, fished, and grew a few crops during the short months of warm weather.

They were people to be avoided, for they were dangerous man-eaters. Their weapons were javelins of whalebone with needlelike points, and they threw these spears with deadly accuracy. They considered human flesh the greatest of delicacies, and ship's masters were warned that they would put in at the island's many coves and harbors at their peril.

Hudson's maps proved to be precise, and he sighted the southern tip of Greenland exactly where he had expected to find it. "Thick ribbed ice," he wrote in his journal, "prevented me from approaching close to the shore. I felt no regrets." He refrained from adding that he was probably thinking about the cannibalism of the natives.

The weather was bitterly cold, but only Greene and Prickett complained, the other members of the company stoically enduring the discomfort. In the days that followed, several mammoth "mountains of floating ice" were seen. Hudson wisely took a course as far from them as possible, having learned that the portion showing above the surface of the sea was only a small fraction of the whole. Even a ship as solidly built as the *Discovery* could be torn to kindling by submerged, jagged-edged mountains of ice.

Thereafter the maps proved unreliable, and Hudson was forced to depend on his own instincts. At last, late in June, he stood off Resolution Island, which both Davys and Sir Martin Frobisher had mentioned in some detail in their logs. He had reached the outer limits of the Furious Overfall, and was so tense he could not sleep. On June 25 the *Discovery* nosed into the Furious Overfall under drastically reduced sail, and immediately was swept along on a swift current.

The Furious Overfall, subsequently named Hudson Strait, holds no mysteries for the modern sailor. The rush of water that puzzled and excited Henry Hudson was—and is—nothing more or less than the swift flow of tides moving in and out of the open Atlantic to the east and Hudson Bay to the west. The strait, four hundred and fifty miles long and approximately one hundred miles wide, is bounded on the north by Baffin Island and on the south by the northern shores of the mainland—the Province of Quebec and Labrador.

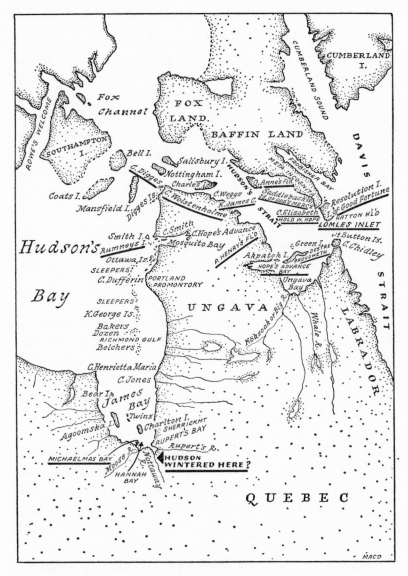

Hudson's fourth and last voyage. Names underlined are those
used by Hudson. Lomles Inlet is the site of the "Furious Overfall" to which the explorer frequently refers.

At no time, either in Hudson's era or in later centuries, has it been a simple matter to sail through the strait. Vast masses of ice, individual icebergs, and smaller floes drift rapidly and erratically, hurled first in one direction and then another by the boiling tides that churn in and out of Hudson Bay. Ordinary compasses—Hudson possessed no other kind—dip wildly because of the strait's proximity to the Magnetic Pole.

The difficulties encountered by the masters of ships employed by the powerful Hudson's Bay Company in the late sixteenth and early seventeenth centuries were so great that specific instructions were issued to all captains. The straits were to be navigated only between July 15 and September 30. The combination of ice and fog made sailing too hazardous the rest of the year.

Hudson, unaware of the problems, entered the straits two weeks early. Fog hid both Baffin Island and the mainland from his lookout, so he had no idea he had entered a channel between two vast bodies of land. Ironically, had he taken Juet back to England, hired another mate, and set out again, he would have reached his Furious Overfall at the right season and would have been able to see both Baffin Island and the mainland.

He plunged westward through turbulent seas, almost blinded by the fog. The tides carried him north, then south again, and his compass was useless. He needed all his skill as a navigator, but soon discovered that the Overfall was too strong for him to continue sailing due west. Doing the best he could under extraordinarily bad sailing weather, he steered toward the south and sighted the Labrador coast. Pushing westward near the broad mouth of what became Ungava Bay in northern Quebec, he passed close to Akpatok Island. Through his glass he saw grapes growing there, but the ice prevented him from landing. On his charts he gave the place the name Desire Provoketh, and in his log he romantically described it as "a champagne land."

In the next two weeks he grimly traveled north, south, and north again, sighting many islands and giving them names, passing from the strait into Ungava Bay and out again. He fought a constant battle against the tides, winds that were as strong as they were fickle, fog that made it impossible to see more than a short distance in any direction, and a damp cold that chilled the entire company to the marrow.

The captain continued to fight his way westward through the strait. He found the experience exhilarating, and was the only member of the company who was not frightened out of his wits most of the time. The crew lived in constant fear, enjoying only short periods of respite. The men became surly, hated their master, and desperately wanted to turn homeward. Gradually, little by little, they were edging toward mutiny.

Fortunately for posterity, several members of the crew recorded their impressions of this period. Prickett kept a lively and colorful diary, Wilson made copious notes, and Greene scribbled his impressions on paper whenever the spirit to write moved him. Juet, of course, continued to keep his usual, methodical diary.

Occasionally, according to Prickett, the ship anchored beside an island of ice during the brief period each day when the sea became quiet. There were pools of clear water, "pure for drinking and good to the taste," on the islands, so the men filled their water casks. Then, alleviating their tension, they raced around on the islands, sliding and falling on the ice as they whooped and chased each other.

Several times, Prickett wrote, they saw huge, shaggy bears, with fur so white that "the beasts approached quite close to us before we could distinguish them from the island snows where they made their nests." One day a party on an ice floe became panicky when a bear started to lumber toward them, moving with great speed in spite of its bulk. The sailors were terrified, for they had left their firearms on board the *Discovery* and knew they were no match for the animal. Someone threw a chunk of ice at the beast, others followed his example, and one caught the bear on the forehead. The startled animal promptly dived into the sea and disappeared as the men scrambled back to the safety of the ship.

But diversions were infrequent and brief. The sea was rough, ice floes were everywhere, and the fog was ever present. Fear mounted, terror became contagious, and the rumor that the captain did not know where he was going swept through the company.

Juet added fuel to the fires of rebellion by openly expressing his contempt for the captain. "A delegation came to me to-day," he wrote in his diary on July 26, "to ask my opinion of our situation. I told them plain that Hudson is a fool. He hopes to reach Bantam in the East Indian Islands by Candlemass, but we shall all be at the bottom of the sea by then if he persists in his madness." With Juet supporting them, the men rebelled and refused to sail any farther.

Henry Hudson's predecessors on the high seas would have taken immediate, personal action to stamp out the mutiny. When reports of the incident later reached London, other masters declared that he should have put a bullet through Juet's head or run the mate through with his cutlass. A direct response of that sort, they said, would have brought the mutiny to an abrupt end.

But the handling of men was the fatal weakness in Hudson's otherwise strong character. Rather than assert himself, punish

Juet drastically, and sail on, he summoned the entire company to a meeting.

There he produced his maps and charts, patiently explaining to the crew that he knew where he was going. He spoke earnestly for more than an hour, and at the end of his talk he demanded, "Tell me yea or nay, you who have wren's hearts, whether you sail with me or would go home." Perhaps it was the worst of his blunders to let the men express themselves, much less vote.

After a long silence, Francis Clemens, the bo's'n, was the first to speak. "If I had one hundred guineas in my purse," he said fervently, "I would gladly give ninety of it to be sitting in my own Dolphin-chamber, at the round table, by a sea-coal fire."

The bo's'n was a man of authority, and the others were impressed. A half-dozen sailors raised their voices to shout that they, too, wanted to go home. Hudson could have stilled the uproar at any time he chose, but he allowed it to continue.

Philip Staffe, the carpenter, was the first to come to the master's defense. "If I had one hundred guineas," he said scornfully, "I would not give ten of it to be back in England, but on the contrary, would consider it as good money as ever I had any."

The captain allowed the argument to rage unchecked. But the elements were active, even if the sailors were not, and ice closed in on three sides. The meeting was adjourned at once, with no final decision reached, and all hands raced up to the deck to work the ship clear of the dangerous floes.

On only one occasion did the company set foot on solid land. Hudson allowed the men to go hunting, hoping that fresh meat would raise their spirits. They flushed out a covey of partridges, but only one bird was shot. Woodhouse, the

Oxford mathematician, who had never handled firearms in his life prior to making the voyage, brought down a bird too old to fly away. It proved inedible.

While the men continued to sulk and debate, Hudson doggedly continued his voyage toward the west. Suddenly, on August 2, 1610, the *Discovery* reached the entrance to a narrow channel. On the left stood a spit of land that the captain called Cape Wolstenholme. Opposite it, approximately two miles away, perhaps a little less, a sheer, vertical cliff soared up more than one thousand feet above the level of the sea. Hudson immediately marked it in his charts as Cape Digges.

The sailors stopped complaining, and even Juet fell silent. Obviously the channel led somewhere, and perhaps the captain was not an idiot after all.

Before proceeding, Hudson anchored in the channel, a difficult feat, and sent three men—Prickett, Bylot, and Greene to Digges Island. They were instructed to climb to the top of the towering cliff and report what they saw ahead.

Prickett wrote about the incident in detail. The sheer face of the cliff made it difficult to land, and a thunderstorm compounded the problem. Finally, however, the gig reached the northern shore of the island, where a small cove loomed ahead, and the landing was made. The men were surprised to find they were on an island. From the channel it had looked like a large body of land. There were many brambles; the ascent was so steep that the men were forced to abandon several attempts to climb the cliff, and their clothes were cut to ribbons. Finally, however, they came to a small river and followed it upstream to the heights. On their climb they saw a herd of deer from a distance, but the animals fled before the sailors could raise their blunderbusses.

Then, at last, they reached a portion sufficiently high to

enable them to look far toward the west. Ahead stood a vast
sea that appeared to be an ocean. Before they could see anything more, the rain stopped and a heavy fog rolled in, making further investigation impossible. The mists were so thick
that the men were guided back to the *Discovery* by the firing
of a pistol every two minutes. After great difficulty they returned to the ship, numbed and frightened by their experience.

Hudson was elated when he heard their story, and felt certain he had reached the Pacific. He was convinced that the
East Indies were ahead to the southwest. He had found the
northwest passage that men had been seeking for so long!
Soon the weather would become balmy, vegetables and fish
and game would be plentiful on scores of lush tropical islands,
and the company's troubles would come to an end.

The trio who had gone ashore on Digges Island begged the
captain to remain anchored until the weather cleared. The
prospect of sailing into another great sea terrified them. But
Hudson laughed and ordered the anchor weighed at once.
Fog or no fog, he intended to push ahead, even though he had
to reduce sail and send a man to the prow to keep a sharp
watch for rocks, ice, and other obstacles.

As soon as the *Discovery* inched into the vast inland sea
later known as Hudson Bay, the entire crew became conscious
of a remarkable phenomenon. For many days they had heard
the constant, menacing growl of ice crunching against ice.
But here there was utter silence. Ice floes drifted apart, and
the captain was convinced that the sea was already becoming
warmer.

He anchored for the night inside the entrance to the bay,
west and south of Cape Wolstenholme. The next morning a
brilliant sun rose in a cloudless sky, and Hudson noted in his
log that the water was as clear as whey.

The *Discovery* sailed south, following the eastern shore of the bay, coming at last to an extension, bounded on the east by Quebec and on the west by Ontario, that is now known as James Bay. To Hudson's intense disappointment, he found that he could proceed no farther south.

His calculations were completely upset. If, as he firmly believed, he had reached the Pacific, there had to be an outlet that would permit him to continue. He explored James Bay thoroughly, sailing in and out, and anchored at least once to send a party ashore for water.

The crew became uneasy again, "concerning our coming into the bay and putting out," Prickett wrote. But Hudson remained seemingly confident. In spite of the obstacles that defied all known data about the surface of the earth, he appeared convinced he would reach the fabulous spice island of Java by the beginning of February.

The captain's surface calm was deceptive, and no one knew it better than Juet, himself a navigator of sufficient experience to read maps. Neither Hudson Bay nor little James Bay, at its southern end, could be found on any chart in the captain's cabin. Juet quietly informed several members of the crew that the *Discovery* was lost. The ship had made her way into unknown waters. The mainland—if indeed it was that large and not an island—might be an unknown continent. Perhaps great glory awaited the intrepid seamen who had made their way into these unknown parts. But dead men could not appreciate posthumous honors. It would be far wiser to return to England at once, before winter came. It was already September, and the *Discovery* was floundering.

This time Juet really went too far. Hudson suspected that Juet's description of the company's situation was accurate. It was true that he could not swear he was in the Pacific. Perhaps he had truly found a new sea and a new continent. But even though he did not know, he was determined to find out. Discovery and exploration meant far more to him—and to all mankind—than the temporary discomfort of his crew.

He called Juet into his quarters and flatly accused the mate of disloyalty. Juet believed the men supported him and brazenly demanded an open trial. This was Hudson's last chance to establish his own ultimate, total authority, based on his position as the ship's master. He made the terrible mistake of believing himself so much in the right that he accepted the challenge, and Juet was tried on September 10 in the presence of the entire company.

The captain treated the mate "with all the etiquette and deference due his rank," Prickett wrote, and allowed him to speak for an hour or more, by the end of which time he had nothing more to say.

Bennett Mathues was the first witness for the prosecution. Juet, he said, had told him when the ship had been drawing near to Iceland that "there would be manslaughter" in the company and that "many would be made bloody."

Several others then swore that after leaving Iceland, Juet had vowed he would turn the ship homeward at the first opportunity. Hudson had not heard this intelligence previously and was surprised by it.

Arnold Lodlo and Philip Staffe took the stand in succession and gave virtually identical testimony. Juet, they declared, had repeatedly urged them to keep unsheathed swords and loaded blunderbusses near their hammocks, telling them an occasion would arise when they would need the weapons for self-protection.

Finally, one sailor after another swore that Juet was to blame for the one serious rebellion that had taken place.

The evidence was overwhelming, and Hudson solemnly announced, "It is fit time to punish and cut off further occasions of the like mutiny." The seamen, made uneasy by the damning revelations of conspiracy, agreed with him.

Hudson took immediate, drastic action. Juet was deposed from his post as mate. After serving a lifetime at sea as an officer, he was made to suffer the disgrace of sailing before the mast as a common, able-bodied seaman. Robert Bylot, whom Hudson considered the best qualified member of the crew to become an officer, was promoted to the rank of mate and was given Juet's wages.

Had Hudson stopped there, all still might have been well. But in his zeal he swept the decks too energetically with his new broom. Francis Clemens, he said, had behaved disloyally during the rebellion and had often encouraged Juet's mutinous talk. Therefore Clemens was also reduced in rank, and William Wilson replaced him as bo's'n. As the captain entertained private doubts about Wilson's abilities, Adrian Motter was made bo's'n's mate. Quartermaster John King and Wilson had comported themselves with such dignity, the master added, that both would be rewarded with a portion of the wages that otherwise would have been paid to the demoted men.

Juet now had Clemens as a firm ally, and no longer stood alone. The captain assured them "that he would be a means for their good, and would forget injuries" if they behaved themselves in the future. But these promises meant nothing to either man. Both knew their sailing days would be terminated when they returned to England. With black marks on their records, no owners or captains would ever want to hire them. With little to lose and much to gain if their mutinous activities could be concealed in some way, the pair now began to conspire in dead earnest.

Equally important, Hudson had allowed the sailors a voice in the proceedings. Just as he had done when he had asked them whether they would accompany him farther, he was permitting his final judgments to be swayed by public opinion. And without realizing it, he had formed the hard core of two opposing groups. Those he had promoted now became "the captain's men," while Juet and Clemens were their unrelenting enemies.

The search of James Bay was resumed as soon as the trial was terminated, but permanent damage had been done. The intellectual Woodhouse, searching for meanings where there were none, confided to several men that he believed the captian wanted to explore the bay "for reasons known only to himself."

Prickett and several others did not have even that much faith in the master. "Up to the north we stood until we raised land," the irritated Prickett wrote in his diary. "Then down to the south we went, and up to the north, then down again to the south in this labyrinth without end."

The men began to wonder why the captain insisted on making these repeated southern probes. A far more sensible procedure, in their opinion, would be to return to the main sea —Hudson Bay—and sail due west. Then they would know for certain whether they were in the Pacific or, perhaps, in a lesser sea that opened onto it.

But the thorough, painstaking Hudson first wanted to satisfy himself that there were no outlets to the south or southwest from the bottom of James Bay. One day, immediately after a storm, he was so anxious to resume his explorations that he ordered the anchor weighed while a very heavy sea was still running. The *Discovery* lurched as the men were hauling up the anchor, and two members of the crew, Adam Moore and Michael Butt, were thrown to the deck, suffering severe bruises. The cable became fouled, too, and the ship might have been damaged had not Philip Staffe cut it free with several heavy ax blows. The whole company was disturbed by the incident.

A few days later they suffered an even more unsettling experience. The *Discovery* finally reached the southwest corner of James Bay, where there were thick swamps. Hudson sent a party ashore in the gig to see if they could find an opening, beyond the marshes, into a larger body of water. The mire became so thick that the men had to climb out into knee-deep cold water as they made their way toward dry land. Suddenly one of them paused and pointed silently. In the mud ahead of them was the clearly defined, bare footprint of a man.

It came as a distinct shock to discover that in this vast, silent wilderness of stunted trees, bramblebushes, and weeds, where the only signs of life had been an occasional wild goose soaring high overhead, there should be other human beings. As the man who had left the print had been barefooted, the sailors assumed that he was a savage. In their nervousness they jumped to the conclusion that the area was inhabited by cannibals.

Finding no water outlet beyond the marsh, the party returned to the *Discovery* and begged the captain to put back out to sea at once before man-eaters swooped down on them out of the wilderness and devoured them. Hudson laughed, which shamed the men.

The captain was still determined to explore every possible outlet to the south, and decided to sail as close to the southern shore of James Bay as he could. Philip Staffe warned him that the bark might strike hidden underwater rocks, but nothing would deter Hudson. Two days later the ship ran up onto a rift and lay there helplessly for twelve hours. Then the wind drove her off, and she escaped with no damage except several gashes in her hull.

The season was now far advanced, and Hudson was compelled to think seriously about going into camp for the winter. There were fine stands of trees in the main bay, to the north, but he realized that by now, in late October, that sea was undoubtedly a solid sheet of ice. The floes were becoming so thick in James Bay itself that he had to sail with great caution.

It took several days to reach the southeast corner of the bay, where there was a small harbor partly sheltered from the winds by three rugged hills. The largest of these was a precipice of four hundred feet. Bare and desolate, it was literally a cliff of sheer granite. The nights were becoming very long, the cold was more bitter each day, and snow fell morning and night.

Hudson realized he could go no farther until spring came. He would not have chosen this barren spot—later known as Rupert Bay—for a semipermanent anchorage, but he no longer had any choice. At least partly because of his lack of foresight, the company would be forced to spend several months in an area devoid of good timber for housing. There was no sign of game anywhere, the men had no luck fishing, and there appeared to be no berries on any bushes for miles around.

Staffe and Prickett were sent ashore to find the best possible place to build a winter camp. Lacking suitable alternatives, they chose the base of the granite hill. Hudson agreed with their reasoning: if nothing else, the hill cut off the sharp north wind.

On November 1 the entire crew went ashore. Lines were attached to the ship, and the men began the backbreaking job of hauling her into shallow water, close to the land. By now the weather was so cold that it became impossible to work for more than short periods. After hauling at the lines for half an hour, men collapsed onto the ground, panting for breath. Some wanted to give in to the desire to stretch out on the hard, snow-packed earth and drift off to sleep. But Hudson, aided by his new mate, Bylot, forced them to their feet again. The captain knew, even if his men did not, that anyone foolish enough to yield to the urge for rest in the open would freeze to death in a few hours.

On November 9 the grueling task of hauling the *Discovery* to a safe, shallow anchorage was completed. That night the temperature fell alarmingly, and when the dawn of a northern winter finally broke on November 10, the men saw that the ice had frozen into a solid mass. No matter what might happen, the ship could not be moved until spring.

The long winter in the wilderness had begun.

X

The Terrible Winter

ॐ

IN EVERY DIRECTION the stranded mariners looked out on a bleak, cheerless landscape. James Bay was frozen solid, with hillocks and mounds of ice and snow rising here and there. These were stained a disagreeable yellow-gray by the salt water. To the west were frozen marshes, and beyond them ice-covered rocks. At the far end of this desolate reach stood some twisted dwarf willows. To the southeast, on the banks of a frozen river that fed into the bay in warmer weather, were miniature juniper, spruce, and pine, all of them so gnarled that Staffe doubted that the wood would be of any value to him for planking, even if he could find some way to thaw it.

Ample supplies of provisions remained in the hold of the *Discovery*. But Hudson spent two days making a careful inventory with his quartermaster, and finally concluded there was not enough food to see the company through the whole winter and a return voyage to England, much less permit further exploration.

Birds unlike any the men had ever seen were nesting in the rocks at the far side of the frozen marsh, and the captain offered the sailors cash awards if they brought in fowl or other game. But, aware of the strong possibility that a man going out alone in the wilderness might freeze to death, he ordered that hunting expeditions be made by at least two men. One, he directed, had to carry a blunderbuss, and the other had to be armed with no weapon smaller than a pike, which could be used to smash holes in ice.

During these first, trying days, John Williams, the ship's gunner, wandered alone into the wilderness, stayed in the open too long, and died of exposure before he could return to the *Discovery*. He was buried in a hole chipped out of the frozen ground, and the captain read several passages from the Bible before everyone hurried back to the ship to escape from the winds.

It had been the custom for more than one hundred years to sell the clothes of an expired seaman to his mates at an auction. As personal belongings were always in short supply, sentiment was not permitted to hinder such a sale. The auction was held, with the captain presiding, but the men were surprised when he failed to put the most valuable item up for bidding. It was a heavy sailor's coat of thick, gray wool, ideal for wear in such a climate.

Hudson explained that he intended to sell the coat to Greene, whose wardrobe was neither ample nor appropriate. Certainly Hudson was within his rights as captain, and his decision was a just one. Nevertheless the men regarded it as another sign of the master's favoritism to Greene, and there was a great deal of muttering behind Hudson's back.

Soon afterward there occurred one of the most unfortunate incidents that had yet taken place. The captain realized that the men were becoming depressed and sour because they were cooped up on board the *Discovery* most of the time. In order to improve their living conditions, he decided to put up a house on shore, using lumber stored in the forward hold. He did not stop to think of the obstacles that would be encountered in construction work at that season. Planks would freeze within a short time after being taken ashore and would become so hard that no nail could be driven into one. A plank dropped onto the ground would stick to the ice and would have to be chipped free. For that matter, nails would become so cold that they would tear skin and flesh from a man's fingers.

Perhaps Hudson knew so little about building that these difficulties did not occur to him. He was at fault, however, for not discussing the subject with Staffe. Instead he sent Bylot to the carpenter with an order to begin construction. Staffe, as moody as anyone else because of the weather, impudently sent back word that he neither could nor would perform the task. He offered no explanation.

Hudson's nerves were ragged, too, and instead of inquiring into the carpenter's reasons, he lost his temper. In Prickett's words, "Captain Hudson ferreted Staffe out of his cabin to strike him, calling him by many foul names, and threatening to hang him."

The conduct of the ship's master on this occasion was inexcusable. No matter what the provocation, captains were required to stand on their dignity at all times, remember their rank, and treat their men fairly.

The burly Staffe refused to accept the abuse meekly. He argued vehemently. He called on the whole company to witness the fact that he was being requested to fulfill an impossible assignment. He declared that he knew far more about his trade than the captain, and ended his own diatribe with the contemptuous assertion that he was "no house carpenter but, by God, a ship's carpenter." The rebuffed Hudson stamped back to his own quarters, still in a fury.

The following day, Staffe—who was probably the best hunter in the company—went ashore to search for game. His companion on this expedition was Henry Greene. As a result, the captain, brooding alone, considered Greene an ingrate who did not deserve his friendship. Foolishly, even stupidly, he promptly sold the gray wool coat of the late John Williams to Bylot. This gesture was so petty and mean that Greene lost his own temper after returning to the ship and loudly demanded that the captain keep his promise.

By now the strain was telling on Hudson, who appeared to lose more self-control with each passing day. He became very angry with the protégé who, until now, could do no wrong. Unless Greene showed him the respect due his rank, he shouted, he would cut off the young man's wages. Adding insult to injury, he also declared that Greene was a conniving rascal and thief whom he would not trust with twenty shillings in silver. Greene, who had spent years living in the jungle of the London underworld, was not one to forgive or forget such talk.

Hudson did show his good sense, however, by patching up his quarrel with Staffe. He apologized to the carpenter in the presence of several other sailors, candidly admitting he had gone too far. Staffe was man enough to shake the captain's hand and admit that he, too, had been wrong. Thereafter the carpenter further demonstrated his mettle by doggedly going to work on shore. With the aid of three others, whom he alternately cajoled and cursed, he managed to overcome staggering odds by building a longhouse somewhat similar to those the captain had seen in his exploration of the Hudson Valley.

Some of the men moved into the dwelling, where a fire blazed day and night. Others preferred to remain on board the *Discovery*. Prickett frankly admitted he was afraid to spend his nights on shore, where cannibals, bears, and other beasts might attack without warning. Every night the men could hear timber wolves howling in the distance, but no member of the crew caught even a glimpse of these dangerous animals. Juet, still determined to stir up trouble, suggested to his superstitious, ignorant mates that the wolves might be supernatural creatures, spawns of Satan who had come to earth to torment mankind. Some of the seamen believed him and refused to walk out of sight of the ship, even in broad daylight.

The diet was monotonous, and as no fruit was available, the men began to suffer from scurvy in January. Their jaws became swollen, their gums rotted; and although they tried drinking melted salt water, at that time the supposed "cure" for the disease, their condition did not improve. In fact, many became ill with stomach complaints because the water from James Bay was brackish. Prickett suffered from a joint ailment, and became so lame he had to fashion himself a crutch of frozen wood to get around. Clemens stayed out in the open too long on a hunting trip one day, and frostbite destroyed his toenails.

Greene now joined the group opposed to the captain. Strangely, his constant companion was the man he had engaged in a fistfight on the beach at Iceland, Edward Wilson, the surgeon. Juet and Clemens remained the master's implacable foes.

Food became increasingly scare as the winter wore on. All birds except the tiny willow-ptarmigan had disappeared, and no matter how many of these small creatures the men brought down and roasted, they complained of constant hunger. Foxes could be heard scampering on the ice near the longhouse at night, and some of the more resourceful seamen set clever traps, but failed to catch even one fox.

Then, out of nowhere, large flocks of geese, swans, and ducks appeared far overhead, flying north. But they proved as elusive as the foxes. They flew too high for the men to shoot them down with blunderbusses, the clumsiest of muskets. On rare occasions some hundreds of birds would glide down to the surface of the frozen bay to rest, but took flight instantly when the stiff-jointed men tried to creep toward them. Yet honking, squawking, and the steady whirring of wings could be heard for hours at a time, tantalizing sailors who were becoming desperate in their yearning for the taste of fresh meat.

Hudson tried to cheer the men. The appearance of the wildfowl, he said, meant that spring would come soon and the travail would end. He had no way of knowing, of course, that the habits of these flocks were unlike those of birds in England and Europe. The weather would not become warmer for many weeks, and in the meantime the birds mysteriously disappeared. The weary, harassed members of the *Discovery*'s crew became increasingly convinced they were living under a dreadful curse.

Food supplies disappeared at a faster rate than Hudson and the quartermaster had calculated. Hunting and fishing parties came back to the winter quarters empty-handed night after disappointing night. "We ate moss," Prickett wrote grimly in his diary, "than which the powder of a post be much better."

At last, however, there were definite signs that spring was approaching. Even though the weather remained bitterly cold,

Prickett noted that "the ice was being exhaled by the sun and sucked full of holes, like honeycomb."

Trees stirred, miraculously showing signs of life. Woodhouse went deep into the woods and came back with two sacks overflowing with buds from a tree no one could identify. Surgeon Wilson boiled the buds, producing an evil-smelling yellow substance. Experiments proved that, when used as a salve, this concoction cured painful skin eruptions. In their desperation the men began to drink the foul brew. To their astonishment their scurvy improved, and painful stomach cramps that had confined many of the sailors to their beds disappeared overnight.

Feeling more like themselves again, although still hungry, the men were further cheered by the realization that the ice was at last breaking up.

One morning the company was electrified when a savage Indian appeared out of the wilderness. Hudson allowed none of his men to move, and made friendly gestures. The warrior was shy, but finally approached. The captain sent Prickett and King to the hold for some knives, hatchets, and mirrors, which the man took, indicating in pantomime that he would return the following day.

He kept his word, hauling a sled on which he had piled several deer skins, two beaver skins, and a side of venison so small that it would scarcely provide the sailors with a single meal. The Indian indicated he wanted to barter, and in sign language convey his desire to trade a deer skin for a hatchet. Hudson insisted that one hatchet was worth two skins. The Indian accepted the bargain with great reluctance.

He went off and was not seen again. Juet murmured to the men that the captain's greed was responsible. Had he treated the native better, the disgraced mate said, other savages would have come to the ship with all the meat the crew could eat. Anxious to put the blame on a scapegoat, some of the seamen agreed.

When most of the ice had disappeared from James Bay, the master sent seven of the crew out in his gig to fish. The party returned at sundown, and for the first time in months the men had cause to cheer. There were at least five hundred fish in the nets, some of them trout, others "a strange sea creature as large as herring and almost as good to the taste."

Perhaps Hudson should have ordered the catch salted at once, but he shared the belief of everyone that the grueling ordeal had come to an end. The men planned a feast, but were dismayed to discover they quickly lost their appetites. Most of the fish were left in mounds on deck.

The next day the fishermen went out again, but enjoyed no luck. Every morning the gig went out at sunrise and did not return until dusk, but no more fish were netted. By the end of a week the better part of the initial catch had spoiled and had to be thrown away.

Greene and William Wilson rashly decided to steal the gig and go off on their own. Somewhere in James Bay, they reasoned, there were fish. The half-starved Greene wrote the captain a farewell note in which he gloated, describing in detail the hundreds of crisply fried fish that he and his single companion would eat.

But the note was never delivered, nor did the plan materialize. The captain happened to arise very early on the morning the men planned to sneak away, and far off to the west, on the shore of James Bay, he saw a column of smoke rising high in the clear air. There were natives—and food—within reach.

Hudson immediately ordered knives, blankets, and beads

piled into the boat. Taking King and two others with him, he dipped into the remaining stocks of food for nine days' worth of provisions and sailed off in the boat, promising to return with ample provisions. He left Bylot in charge during his absence, and was so eager to leave that he set no date for his return.

The next week was the most frustrating he had yet known. Repeatedly he caught glimpses of the Indians in the distance, but they fled whenever he tried to approach them. On one occasion, when he tried to follow them into the wilderness, they set fire to a large patch of forest in order to protect their rear as they escaped.

Meanwhile Bylot was finding it difficult to establish his authority over men who, until recently, had been his equals. Perhaps the newly appointed mate did not try hard enough to preserve discipline when the sailors demanded extra food. They were tired of living on reduced rations, they said, and preferred to eat their fill immediately, taking their chances on starving to death later. Bylot succumbed to their demands, and ate as much as anyone else.

The exhausted, discouraged captain returned at the end of seven days. Hudson was stunned when he discovered that the larder had been so heavily raided. He put the full blame on Bylot, and instantly demoted the one capable seaman who had remained loyal to him. Then he chose John King as his new mate, and could not have made a worse selection. King was unquestionably loyal, but had little else to recommend him for the post. He was slow of speech, incapable of making up his mind swiftly, and had no experience as a navigator. Later it was claimed that he could neither read nor write, an allegation that is scarcely credible as he had been hired originally as quartermaster, a post that required literacy.

Regardless of whether the claim is true, King was a poor choice. No one trusted his ability to handle the ship and, consequently, no one respected him as an officer. Equally significant, Bylot now joined the growing ranks of the disaffected.

When the *Discovery* finally weighed anchor to sail north out of James Bay on June 12, she had spent seven and one-half months in winter quarters. Provisions were running alarmingly low. No one knew for certain how much food was left, as the captain now kept the key to the storage cabins himself and permitted no one to enter them with him. At least half the crew had grievances against him, some justified, some imaginary. The men were exhausted. They had no heart for fresh adventures and were afraid that, even if they sailed for England immediately, they would starve before they reached home.

Hudson was worried about the lack of provisions, and as he was aware of the men's discontent, he took what he believed to be the only steps possible to alleviate the situation. On the morning of the last day at anchor in James Bay he sent several of the sailors in the gig to try their luck at fishing for the last time. They came back with approximately eighty small fish, which were consumed at a single sitting.

Then, on the morning of June 12, he went into the storage cabins and brought out all the remaining bread and cheese. Each man's share amounted to approximately one pound of bread and seven of cheese. The captain distributed the entire amount, explaining that each man would be responsible for his own provisions. Several privately thought him weak because he wept when he handed out the pitifully inadequate rations of bread.

Hudson realized that some of the cheese was spoiled, and thought that, by giving each seaman his fair share of both good and bad, he would prevent future problems. His motives were good, but the results were catastrophic. First, a rumor swept through the company that he was holding back large quantities of cheese for his own use. In addition, some sailors were so lacking in will power that they were unable to ration themselves. Green ate all of his cheese in two days. William Wilson made a glutton of himself and devoured his entire consignment in a few hours, with the result that he spent the next three days in his hammock, suffering violent cramps.

Mutual suspicions made it almost impossible to attain harmony. Juet continued to whisper that the captain was hoarding food for his own use. Hudson, for his part, believed that the men were concealing bread in their personal belongings. Apparently he was convinced that someone had broken into the storage cabins, for his shock and dismay had been genuine when he had discovered how little was left.

Hoping to find the culprit, he sent Nicholas Syms to search through the company's seabags. "Thirty small cakes" were found, but nothing else, and the search was abandoned. The resentment of the men became even more intense, and they told each other that the captain had no right to touch their private property. Virtually the entire company was skirting the thin ice of open mutiny.

At this critical moment, as the *Discovery* was slowly sailing north from James Bay into Hudson Bay, a climactic incident caused a new uproar. William Wilson, recovered from his indigestion, went up onto the deck for some fresh air to help clear his head. He saw Philip Staffe standing alone near the prow, and something in the carpenter's manner seemed strange. Wilson joined him, and saw that Staffe was "eating a large chunk of the beef that had been pickled in England and that we had thought long since eaten."

Wilson immediately wanted to know where Staffe had found the meat. The honest carpenter replied that the captain had given it to him.

"Why should the master so favor to give meat to some of the company, and not to the rest?" Wilson demanded, according to Prickett's diary.

The carpenter's reply confirmed the sailors' deepest suspicions. "It is necessary that some should be kept up," he supposedly said.

Whether Staffe was really eating meat and was sufficiently ingenuous to admit that the captain was favoring some members of the crew is a mystery that has never been solved. Perhaps Wilson made up the story to justify the tragic events of the next few days. It is still more likely that the entire tale was the product of Prickett's lively imagination. His diary for this period, the only document that gives a full account of the events that took place on the night of June 23 and the dark days that followed, is so glib, clever, and sanctimonious that his honesty is open to question.

Regardless of whether Staffe actually was eating food given to him privately by the captain, Hudson himself undoubtedly sparked the ultimate tragedy.

Certainly he knew the men were ravenously hungry. He knew, too, that most of them hated him. He also realized that they were yearning with all their hearts to return to England. They were sick of adventure, indifferent to discovery, and uninterested in exploration. They could think only of going home.

Henry Hudson had suffered privations as great as those endured by his men, but he was no ordinary mortal. When the *Discovery* swept into Hudson Bay under full sail, and he saw a great sea of sparkling, clear blue water, he was revitalized.

All the cares of the difficult autumn, frightful winter, and grueling spring were forgotten. Here was a vast, unknown body of salt water.

Perhaps, by sailing west, he would reach the fabled Spice Islands of the Orient. At the very least, he believed, he would be able to locate the elusive channel that would take him into the Pacific Ocean. His lifelong passion flamed anew, and he was determined to find the northwest passage.

The sailors were horrified when, on the morning of June 23, the captain ordered them to sail due west. Several begged him to reconsider, but he was deaf to their pleas. He had set out from England on a specific mission, and nothing would persuade him to change his mind or alter his course. Food would be found, he insisted, although he knew neither where nor how. Cutting short the discussion, he walked alone to the far side of the quarterdeck.

The men obeyed him silently. But there was something sinister in the sullen glances they exchanged. Throughout the day they gathered in small groups of two and three, muttering in low tones, looking over their shoulders to make sure they were not overheard.

The *Discovery* company had reached the breaking point.

XI

Mutiny

ह∾

AT SUNDOWN on June 23, the *Discovery* anchored for the
night in a sea filled with small ice floes. After an inadequate
meal, the hungry, weary men went off to their hammocks in
the fo'c'sle, where a series of partial bulkheads divided the
living quarters of the crew. There, when the majority had
settled down for the night, Henry Greene and William Wilson slipped into the cubicle occupied by Abacuk Prickett.

Swearing the former valet to secrecy, they told him that in
another two weeks there would be no provisions left. But,
they said, the captain was mad and refused to take the starving sailors home. Therefore, Greene and Wilson declared,
they were determined to take matters into their own hands,
even though it meant committing the greatest crime on the
high seas, mutiny. They planned to put Hudson into the gig
with his supporters and the sick who could no longer func-
tion, "and let them shift for themselves."

"We are ready," Greene said, "and will either succeed or die."

Prickett, according to his diary, pleaded with them. "Do not commit so foul a thing in the sight of God and man as that would be," he begged.

Greene cut him short. It was true, he said, that they might hang, but he preferred the gallows to starvation.

Then the conspirators informed Prickett that the mutineers had voted him a place in their ranks. In his written account, at least, he professed to be horrified, and allegedly was told he would either join the band or be forcibly put into the gig with the other victims.

Juet suddenly appeared at the cubicle opening. The wily old dissembler believed that cajolery was more effective than threats, and assured Prickett that the others had put their case crudely. Hudson and those who would be ejected from the ship with him would not be treated badly. Now that summer was approaching, there would be game and berries in the forests, fish in the sea. The men in the gig would not starve. Eventually they would be able to make their way to the fishing fleets off the shores of Newfoundland. The drastic measures being planned were a form of self-preservation, and nothing else. Certainly no one would be murdered. And, the glib Juet concluded, he knew beyond all doubt that the conspirators would be exonerated when they reached England.

Prickett knew his own situation was hazardous. If he refused to become a member of the band, he would be cast into the gig. If he tried to warn the captain, he would be killed before he could reach Hudson's quarters.

So, according to his diary, he had to content himself with a compromise. He would take no active part in the uprising, but would not oppose it, either, provided that each of the conspirators would take an oath on the Bible that they would not commit murder.

Juet promptly agreed.

Prickett then requested that each of the mutineers come to him in turn and repeat, "I swear truth to God, my Prince and country. I shall do nothing but to the glory of God and the good of the action in hand, and harm to no man."

Juet, Greene, and Wilson took the oath and crept away. A few moments later John Thomas and Michael Perse came to Prickett. Then Adrian Motter and Bennett Mathues appeared.

The story has a hollow, unconvincing ring. Prickett failed to explain why the conspirators should have been so anxious to seek his cooperation, or why they should have been willing to take an oath devoid of meaning.

His factual account of what happened during the rest of the night sounds more like the truth. The mutineers were afraid that King, the new mate, might be conferring with the captain in the master's quarters. If the two officers were together, there might be trouble, as it would be far more difficult to subdue two armed men than one. Eventually it was learned, however, that the mate was on deck, talking with Philip Staffe.

One of the conspirators silently followed King back to his quarters and took up guard outside his closed door. Greene, Hudson's former protégé, stationed himself outside the captain's cabin. Staffe was sleeping on deck, and two men went to keep a nervous watch over him. The mutineers were not certain whether he would stand with them or oppose them. If he remained loyal to the captain, he would be dangerous because of his tremendous physical strength.

Bond, the cooper, was crippled as a result of frostbite. Woodhouse was ill, and Fanning had become lame as the result of a mysterious bone ailment in both his legs. All three were marked for extermination. The mutineers ruthlessly planned to let only the fit survive.

The night passed very slowly. Shortly before dawn Robert Bylot went from cubicle to cubicle in the fo'c'sle to insure that all was in readiness, and Prickett learned for the first time that the man who had served as mate for a short time was one of the ringleaders.

Dawn broke, and Mathues went to the water butts with a kettle, a chore he performed every morning before cooking breakfast. This was the signal to begin operations.

Bylot, seeking revenge on his successor, quietly tapped on King's door. When the sleepy mate appeared, Bylot told him there seemed to be a small fire in the forward hold. King ran there, with Bylot at his heels. As soon as the mate went into the hold, Bylot slammed the door behind him and secured it with a bolt.

At the same time, Greene went up onto the deck to divert Staffe's attention. Two other mutineers remained in the shadows, ready to dispose of the carpenter if he became violent.

King pounded on the door of the hold in impotent rage, and the sound aroused the captain. Perhaps he suspected that something was amiss, for he emerged from his quarters with a cutlass in his hand. But he had no chance to use his weapon. Mathues and John Thomas jumped on him, and William Wilson came up behind him, caught him around the neck, and bore him to the deck. Before he had time to realize what was happening, he was securely trussed with a length of strong line.

Surgeon Edward Wilson heard the noise, opened his door, and called out to ask what was happening. Hudson replied that he had been bound hand and foot.

Two of the mutineers immediately went to the surgeon and asked if he felt well. He replied that he did. Mathues told him that "if he were well he should keep himself so." The surgeon quietly closed his door.

Hudson demanded to know his captors' intentions, and they replied that he would find out when he was in the gig.

The events that took place in the next quarter of an hour were wildly confused. Men who had been active in the conspiracy now became its victims. Others, who had been marked for death, actively joined the mutineers. Judging from Prickett's written account and the testimony later given in England by the survivors, there was no clear-cut plan of action from this time.

Bylot, who remained below so he could not be accused of having attacked the captain, subsequently declared that he believed the mutineers merely intended to place Hudson in the gig, search the ship for supplies they thought he had secreted, and then let him return to his post.

Juet, Greene, and William Wilson were in charge, but their authority was divided. The gig was lowered into the water. Mathues and Thomas carried Hudson down to it. At this point Greene apparently decided that it might be wise to eliminate two such dangerous, rough men, and intended to force them to remain there.

Clemens demurred, however, and was supported by Bond, who had become an active participant in the mutiny, even though he had been listed as an occupant of the gig. Thomas and Mathues climbed onto the deck and forced two of their fellow conspirators, Michael Butt and Arnold Lodlo, to take their places in the boat. Perhaps they carried personal grudges against the pair and decided at the last moment that they should perish. The sudden assault on them makes little sense, and no explanation was offered for this dramatic act of double treachery.

John Hudson, struggling bravely, was compelled to descend into the gig. Fanning, too weak to argue, was lowered into the boat. So was Adam Moore, who had the misfortune to fall sick during the night and awaken in the morning with a raging fever. Woodhouse protested loudly as he was carried to the boat. He promised to give the mutineers all his worldly goods if they would let him remain on board, and swore his family would reward them handsomely if they allowed him to accompany them to England. His pleas were ignored.

Meanwhile Juet went down to the hold to bring King up to the deck. A surprise awaited the old man when he slid back the bolt on the door of the hold. King leaped out, a cutlass in his hand. The mutineers had forgotten that spare weapons were stored in the hold, and the mate had been able to arm himself.

With one blow he knocked Juet's sword from his hand. The old man backed off down the narrow passageway as King advanced, intending to run him through. At that moment several of the conspirators, who had become impatient at the delay, hurried below to see what was happening. The combined efforts of three men were required to subdue King, take him up to the deck, and force him into the gig.

There remained only Philip Staffe, who had stood quietly on deck throughout the mutiny, three conspirators ready to attack him if he tried to help the captain. The mutineers hoped Staffe would join them, as he was the most skilled artisan in the entire crew. But in this moment of supreme crisis, Staffe's honor proved stronger than his desire to abandon his captain.

"I will not stay in this ship unless you force me to stay," he declared suddenly, speaking in a loud voice. "Give me my tools, and may your souls be damned for all Eternity. For the love of God and the master I will go down into the boat rather than accept of likelier hopes with such villains."

Several of the conspirators tried to dissuade him, but Staffe caught hold of Mathues and said he wanted to hear no more talk. His huge fist clenched, he was prepared to smash Mathues' face to a pulp, and he showed no fear of the mutineers' firearms, swords, and knives.

The mutineers were awed by Staffe's demonstration of courage. Someone went below for his chest of tools and an iron cooking pot. The carpenter took them, contemptuously thrust Mathues aside, and climbed down into the gig of his own free will. One of the men threw him a blunderbuss, another promised him ammunition and powder before the gig was cut loose, and still another tossed him a small bag of wheat flour.

With Juet and Bylot on the quarterdeck, the *Discovery* weighed anchor, hoisted her sails and started to pick her way through the ice floes.

The gig was in tow behind the ship, and Henry Hudson stood proudly erect, Staffe beside him. The master was still wearing his dressing robe, "a motley gown," and seemed unaware of the bitter cold.

Prickett, discreetly remaining in his quarters, opened a porthole and called out to the captain that Greene, not Juet, was basically responsible for the mutiny.

Hudson made no reply.

Slowly the mutineers steered toward the open sea. As they approached it, one of the men kept the promise to Staffe and threw him a bag containing a few bullets and a small quantity of gunpowder.

Then the line was cut, and the gig was cast adrift. The

Discovery headed out toward the open sea and immediately sailed in the direction of the east coast of Hudson Bay.

Henry Hudson, his young son, and seven sailors were abandoned to the elements and the wilderness. Prickett wrote in his diary, "They were without food, drink, fire, clothing, or other necessaries."

Several of the mutineers continued to watch the gig as it grew smaller in the distance. Hudson and Staffe hoisted the boat's sail, and the captain made a vain attempt to follow the ship. Displaying consummate skill, he managed to leave the ice field and reach the clear, open water. But he gradually fell farther and farther behind, unable to match the sailing speed of the larger vessel. At noon, perhaps a little earlier, the gig became a tiny dot on the horizon and then disappeared from view.

Henry Hudson and his companions in the gig were never seen again. Their fate is unknown. In the years that followed, countless stories were told, and legends abound.

According to one tale, the master of an English merchant ship reached the southeast corner of Hudson Bay in the summer of 1629. He sent his men ashore for water, and there they found a cabin that had been constructed of planks cut with a carpenter's tools. Several beds of pine boughs lined the inner walls of the building, and a rusted iron cooking pot stood just inside the entrance. But there was no sign of clothing or of a blunderbuss. The ship's master and his men made a thorough search of the area, but found neither any living humans nor any skeletal remains of the great explorer and his fellow sufferers.

The story itself is suspect. William Connor, the master of the *Swallow*, was a debt-ridden, heavy drinking seaman who undertook his voyage in the hope of finding gold or silver in the great bay that Henry Hudson had discovered. The undertaking was a miserable failure, and many of his contemporaries believed he invented the story as a means of winning favorable publicity and obscuring his insolvency. Some members of his crew supported his tale, but others declared that the cabin and its contents were a figment of Connor's imagination.

When he was asked why he had not brought the kettle with him as proof of his find, Connor's answers were vague, evasive, and thoroughly unsatisfactory.

Other travelers who visited Hudson Bay in the quarter of a century that followed the cruel abandonment of the nine men in the gig also returned to England with elusive, fragmentary stories. Some told of seeing blue-eyed men with shaggy hair, dressed in deerskins, who apparently lived like animals and fled into the wilderness at the approach of English sailors. Others claimed to have seen broken bits of Philip Staffe's tools.

One account, more ingeniously inventive than the rest, declared that the master of a ship went ashore in Hudson Bay to hunt for game. He brought down a deer with a single musket shot, and to his amazement found that the animal had been previously injured by a bullet wound in the flesh of its side, but had survived. The bullet fired by a blunderbuss, was still lodged in the animal's side, but it was not carried to England as proof of the tale.

In 1670 the Hudson's Bay Company was formed when King Charles II granted a charter to his cousin, Prince Rupert, and seventeen other gentlemen-financiers. Rupert of the Rhine was one of the most remarkable men of the seventeenth century. A distinguished cavalryman, he became commander-in-chief of the armies loyal to Charles I during the Great Rebellion. After the unfortunate Charles lost his head, Rupert became a great seaman, and eventually turned pirate, for a time, to finance the Stuart cause of Charles II.

After the restoration of the Stuarts in 1660, Rupert stood high in his cousin's favor, serving first as admiral of the fleet and, subsequently, as First Lord of the Admiralty. A genius who invented a new type of brass for cannon and a new type of gunpowder, Rupert was an artist of extraordinary talent, an explorer—and a great admirer of the discoverer-explorers who had preceded him. He was fascinated by the mystery of Henry Hudson's disappearance, and decided to make a determined effort to learn Hudson's fate.

One of the first ships sent out by Rupert after the formation of the Hudson's Bay Company was specifically directed to hunt down every clue. The master of the vessel, Captain Edwin Edwards, was bold, resourceful, and intelligent. He followed the course Hudson had taken in the *Discovery*, and after studying prevailing winds and tides in late June, went ashore for a thorough investigation at all the places he believed Hudson might have landed.

Edwards and his crew spent more than a year in Hudson's Bay, arriving there on June 15, 1674, and remaining until late July, 1675. They returned to England full of admiration for Hudson, having themselves spent a winter in the icy wilderness. But they found no scrap of evidence, no hint of Hudson's fate.

Not until 1725 was the silence broken. In that year an agent of the Hudson's Bay Company named Miller wrote to London headquarters that a Cree Indian with "surprisingly pale skin" who came to a company post to trade furs boasted that one of his ancestors had been an Englishman. The Indian declared that his ancestor had been one of a "few" Englishmen living in the forest. This man, the only survivor of the group, joined the Cree, became one of them, and eventually took a Cree wife.

It is possible that this Englishman might have been Hudson or one of his companions in misery. On the other hand, the Indians of the region well might have heard of Henry Hudson's disappearance. And, with the amiability of a savage telling a story he knew his auditor wanted to hear, the Cree could have invented the entire tale out of whole cloth.

This tantalizing story, like those that preceded it, is too inconclusive to indicate authoritatively what actually became of Hudson, his son, Staffe, and the other unfortunates. Perhaps they were drowned in the waters of the great bay. Perhaps they went ashore and starved to death. Perhaps they were killed by savages.

The truth has been locked for more than three and one-half centuries in the silent wilderness that Henry Hudson discovered—and that claimed him as its own.

XII

The Fruits of Villainy

 કૈ≥

ROBERT BYLOT was elected master of the *Discovery* by the
company of mutineers and took charge of the ship. It is
curious that Juet, who had served as an officer for a lifetime,
was distrusted by the men. He had engaged in so many con-
spiracies over so long a time that none of the others trusted
him, and the most they would grant him was the restoration
of his onetime rank as mate.

No sooner did the gig disappear from sight than the men
shortened sail and, leaving Bylot alone on the quarterdeck,
ransacked the ship. First they looted the personal belongings
of all whom they had forced overboard, quarreling violently
over the shirts, shoes, and other belongings they hauled from
the seabags of their victims. They went through all of the
captain's property, too, but were curiously reluctant to steal
it. In the back of every mutineer's mind, apparently, there

loomed the shadow of the inquiry that inevitably would be held when and if they reached England.

They did find a quantity of food in Hudson's private store, however, and had no qualms about appropriating it. Prickett mentioned two hundred biscuits, a cask of beer and several jars of brandywine. Wilson, Green, and Thomas, the ringleaders of the conspiracy, drank freely before breaking into the food storage cabins that the captain had always kept locked.

There they were overjoyed to discover far more food than they had hoped to find. There were barrels of flour and pork, a half-bushel of dried peas, and two casks of butter, as well as smaller amounts of beef, oatmeal, and barley. These provisions, Prickett reasoned in his diary, had been held in reserve by Hudson for emergency use during his search for the northwest passage.

Prickett's own situation rapidly became precarious. Regardless of whether he had taken part in the mutiny from the start or had been forced to become an accomplice, as he wrote in his diary, he was sufficiently intelligent to realize that authorities in England would make life difficult for the survivors.

So, taking his life in his hands, he begged the others to turn back and pick up the men they had abandoned. Greene and Thomas drove him below deck at pistol point, and Greene made it clear that he was being allowed to live for only one reason. He was clever, and he could write. Therefore he would keep a journal that would exonerate the crew if they should be tried for their crimes.

William Wilson was even more vehement. His breath reeking of strong brandywine, the burly sailor swore that, rather than face a court of snooping officials, he and his companions would become freebooters. Any man who disagreed, he declared, would be thrown overboard into the sea.

Wilson's diatribe was cut short by a shout from one of the men who had gone up to the deck. The gig had appeared again on the horizon and was rapidly gaining on the *Discovery*. All hands forgot loot and their own quarrels to scramble up into the rigging. Soon the ship was moving again under full sail.

Whether the gig was actually sighted again remained a mystery. Bylot, who was in a better position than any of his companions to know the truth, later gave sworn testimony that the gig was sailing toward the southern shore of the bay when he had last seen her.

In any event, the seamen wanted to leave the area as soon as possible, and headed north along the eastern shore of Hudson Bay. Food was still a major worry, and after two days of flight, the *Discovery* anchored off the shore of an island to fish. But there were so many rocks beneath the surface of the water that the mutineers enjoyed no luck. Bylot then nosed into a tiny, natural harbor, and several of the men went ashore. Michael Perse shot two ducks, and others gathered large handfuls of herbs and weeds, which were boiled with the ducks to make a none too nourishing soup.

The ship remained in the harbor for a night and most of another day, waiting to see if the gig was still in pursuit. There was no sign of her, however, and the ringleaders breathed more easily.

The voyage was resumed, and Greene utilized his experience in the London underworld to good advantage. He bullied his companions, frightening some and cowing the majority. Although he was incapable of sailing a ship, he insisted that the others call him "Captain." He appropriated Hudson's boots, his good suit of velvet and another of wool, and a silk-lined cape. Oddly, he took care not to touch any of the master's weapons.

One of Greene's first acts was to place Prickett in charge of the captain's log and journal, with instructions to destroy anything Hudson had written that might incriminate the mutineers. Prickett obeyed, if for no other reason than because he had his own neck to protect. Greene's ability to read and write was limited, and both Wilson and Thomas were illiterate, so the wily Prickett could have spared most of the log and journal had he wished. But, concerned with what a board of inquiry would find, he ruthlessly destroyed large portions of both accounts.

Greene also directed that Juet, whom he completely distrusted, should neither have access to the documents nor be permitted to enter the master's quarters for any purpose, at any time.

After a few days Bylot and Juet, the only members of the company who understood anything about navigation, began to bicker. Bylot insisted that the eastern shore of the bay be kept in sight at all times. Juet, who was far more experienced, said that too much ice was piled up in that direction, and proposed that the *Discovery* sail toward the open seas of the northwest. Bylot refused to take his advice, and soon drifting ice hemmed in the ship on all sides. There was ice, Prickett wrote, "that continued miles and half-miles in every direction about us."

The *Discovery* was a prisoner of the ice floes for two weeks, but finally Bylot managed to work her free when the weather became a little warmer. Even now, however, he stubbornly refused to listen to Juet and continued to keep the eastern shore in sight.

Prickett learned that Greene disliked him and had wanted to put him into the gig, but had been dissuaded by others who valued the former valet's ability to read and write. Prickett wrote in his diary that he was afraid his days might be numbered, and he bitterly regretted the mutiny.

The ship sailed so close to a cluster of four islands that Bylot was able to anchor near to the shore of the largest. Five of the mutineers went up onto the rocky island, but found no game and no birds. They returned to the ship with some handfuls of herbs, and were greeted by their companions with groans.

At this period Bylot began to keep his own log. When Greene heard of it he became alarmed and forced Bylot to swear that he would remain at sea until the company received a written pledge bearing the seal of King James that no one would be prosecuted. Bylot took the oath, but Greene was not completely satisfied. There was little that Greene could do, however, to insure that Bylot kept his word. The title of "Captain" was an empty honor, Greene was learning. He and his friends had the power to throw Bylot overboard, but that would leave only the unreliable Juet to sail the ship.

There were more immediate worries than the potential severity of royal justice to occupy the entire company for the present. One morning the *Discovery* rammed an underwater rock but managed to stay afloat. The men had no boat to investigate the damage, but as nearly as they judge, it was inconsequential.

Then they saw land to the north, and some of the men thought they were coming, at long last, to the channel between the two great cliffs that led into the sea. They were bitterly disappointed when, a few hours later, they found that the land to the north was just a cape jutting out from the eastern shore. At least half the company, Green included, became hysterical and insisted that the *Discovery* was lost. Juet, who had been drinking heavily, supported their claim.

But Bylot refused to change course. Prickett, who went with him into Hudson's cabin to study the master's maps and charts, agreed that Bylot was right. They stood alone against all the others.

Hoping to give the men something useful to do, Bylot suggested that they make a new boat out of lumber stored in the hold. At first Greene opposed the idea but finally agreed when Bylot explained that it would be far easier to go ashore on islands to search for food if a small craft were available. The sailors went to work and fashioned a crude boat that was little better than a raft. Philip Staffe's skills were sorely missed.

Twice Bylot anchored off an island, and twice the men went ashore. But both times they returned with nothing except masses of herbs, which they boiled and greedily ate. The specter of starvation loomed larger.

Finally, when everyone except Bylot and Prickett had abandoned hope of survival, the twin cliffs of Cape Digges and Cape Wolstenholme were sighted ahead. The hungry, exhausted men cheered hoarsely and gazed with hungry eyes at the thousands of birds that rose from the cliffs and circled high overhead.

On the afternoon of July 26 Bylot drove the ship through the opening of the narrow channel that would take the *Discovery* back into the Atlantic. But the tides were too tricky for a relatively inexperienced navigator to handle the ship, and the *Discovery* ran onto a rock. She lay there, leaning helplessly to starboard, through the long hours of the night. Once again the men became hysterical, afraid they would perish. Greene and Wilson became embroiled in such a violent argument that others had to intervene before they killed each other.

Then, suddenly, a "flood" from the west, five fathoms high, roared into the channel and set the ship free. By daybreak she had passed through the strait.

That morning Bylot anchored, taking care not to venture too close to shore for fear that the Furious Overfall would smash the ship on the rocks. The crude boat was lowered, and the sailors who manned it spent hours rowing it toward the cliffs. They landed, caught thirty birds, and then spent an even longer time rowing back to the ship, where they sprawled in exhaustion.

On July 28 Bylot sailed north of the channel, hoping to find the place where a party had gone ashore previously and found the gulls' breeding place. He maneuvered closer, expecting to anchor, when suddenly a large number of savages appeared in a fleet of canoes, two of them very large, the others rather small. In all, there were at least sixty warriors in the party.

Both groups were surprised, but the natives reacted more quickly. Their smaller canoes were hauled into their larger craft. Then, with their company consolidated, they approached the *Discovery* in a friendly manner. They pointed toward Digges Island, indicating in pantomime that they wanted to meet the strangers on shore.

Greene was suspicious, but finally ordered that Prickett, whom he considered expendable, go down into the lead canoe. Then the crude boat was lowered into the water and manned by heavily armed sailors. One of the natives climbed onto it, and with each group holding a hostage, both parties went ashore.

The natives' tents stood in a semicircle behind the beach of a small cove, and the savages appeared completely friendly. They led the strangers to the nesting birds and proudly demonstrated their ability to capture gulls with an ingenious contraption consisting of a long pole to which a rawhide noose was attached.

Wilson was determined to show his superiority to savages, and fired his blunderbuss, killing eight birds. The savages were duly impressed. Both groups caught large numbers of gulls, and for the first time in months the sailors had reason to believe they would not sleep on empty stomachs that night. The united party went back to the cove together, and there the savages entertained their visitors with a dance. At its conclusion they gave the Englishmen gifts of furs and tusks of walrus ivory.

Whether these natives were coastal members of the Cree tribe or Eskimos has never been determined. Prickett wrote in his diary that they were "big-boned, broad-faced, flat-nosed, and small-footed, like the Tartars." No other description has survived.

The sailors went back to the boat, believing their famine was ended at last. Greene had arranged to go ashore again in the morning, promising to bring the natives gifts in return for vension. He had noted that native women were roasting whole sides of meat over open fires, and appeared to possess great quantities of it.

In the morning the three ringleaders—Greene, Wilson, and Thomas—went ashore in the boat, taking Perse, Motter, and Prickett with them. Prickett, who limped heavily, would be used again as a hostage if it proved necessary, but the sailors expected no treachery. The savages had proved companionable, and the whole group, with the exception of Prickett, enjoyed the outing. In the boat were piles of mirrors, bells, and other trinkets, which had been taken from the large supply stored in Hudson's quarters.

The natives were waiting at their camp, and Prickett was left in the boat while the others went ashore. Perse and Motter climbed up onto rocks to gather sorrel, which grew in abundance there. Greene, Wilson, and Thomas took a few trinkets with them and began to barter.

Prickett, watching them from the boat, was surprised to see that the savages had no supplies of venison on hand. He heard Greene inquire at some length about the meat, illustrating his words with broad gestures. The natives pointed toward the forest behind them, and called to their dogs, "a fierce breed of beast that ran up and down the beach in large numbers."

A savage started to wade out toward the boat, and Prickett lost interest in what was happening on the beach. Something in the man's manner made him uneasy, and he waved the native back. The man pretended to misunderstand, but Prickett waved more vehemently, and at last the man turned way. At that moment Prickett caught a glimpse of a second savage climbing up onto the boat behind him.

The warrior held a knife poised over his head, and struck just as Prickett turned. Prickett raised his right arm instinctively, and deflected the blow. But the savage struck a second time, then a third, inflicting a severe gash in Prickett's thigh and almost cutting off the little finger of his left hand.

But Prickett did not give up easily. His arms and hands were powerful, and in spite of his wounds he grappled with his assailant. They struggled silently on the rocking boat, and at last Prickett was able to free his right hand. He snatched his own knife from his belt and slashed his enemy's throat. The savage fell back, unconscious.

Meanwhile the other natives had launched a simultaneous attack on the other mutineers. Heavily outnumbered, the quintet had no opportunity to draw their pistols. William Wilson and John Thomas suffered far greater pain than would have been inflicted on them by King James' magistrates. They were disemboweled, and fell to the ground, "screaming in agony as they expired."

Greene was wounded, as was Perse, but both managed to scramble down to the boat, with the savages in pursuit. Prickett shoved off, and with a single oar slowly maneuvered the boat into deeper water.

Motter, who had wandered higher onto the rocks to search for sorrel, saw what was taking place below. He leaped into the icy water and swam to the boat.

He and several of the warriors reached it simultaneously. Greene smashed the heads of two natives with a pike, and Perse split open the head of another with his hatchet. Prickett was trying desperately to turn the boat away from the shore, but could not accomplish the feat alone.

Perse managed to haul Motter into the boat, then left the half-drowned man and the wounded Greene to deal with the other savages who were still thrashing in the water, trying to climb into the craft. Prickett was still working feverishly and, aided now by Perse, succeeded in turning the boat around. Motter and Perse leaped to the oarsmen's seats, almost upsetting the ungainly boat, and began to row frantically out of the harbor. Greene and Prickett beat off the savages who continued to cling to the stern, and it appeared as though the mutineers' chances of escaping from the cove were improving.

Ironically, no one on board the *Discovery* was aware of what was taking place in the harbor, as the high rocks made it impossible to see the cove from the ship's anchorage. New dangers beset the frantic men in the boat. Savage archers began to fire at them, and other natives ran to their canoes, intending to pursue the battered company.

The marksmanship of the Indians was deadly. Greene's pistol failed to fire, and as he hastily knocked out the charge of damp gunpowder and tried to reload the weapon, an arrow cut into his stomach, doubling him over. The pain was so intense that he screamed, but the sound was swallowed up in the silence of the wilderness. Then a second arrow penetrated his chest, and he babbled incoherently, his head drooping over the stern. A few moments later he was dead. Henry Hudson's principal executioner had paid a frightful penalty for his crime.

Prickett made an attempt to haul Greene's body back into the boat. He was partly turned toward the shore when an arrow lodged in his back. He was fortunate that it did not strike a vital organ, but he was in great pain. With rare presence of mind he managed to pull the weapon out and bled heavily.

Then an arrow struck Perse, but he continued to row until the boat cleared the harbor and stood out to sea. His exertions finally proved too great, and he slumped over in a faint.

Motter, chilled to the bone by his plunge in the icy water, was the only man in the craft who had been neither wounded nor killed. He stood, waving an oar above his head in an attempt to attract the attention of the sailors on board the *Discovery*. But no one noticed him until two canoes filled with savages shot out of the harbor in pursuit of the boat.

Then, at last, Bylot realized something out of the ordinary

was taking place. The smaller of the ship's cannon was fired, and the roar of the gun was so loud that the natives immediately turned back to their cove. Thousands of frightened gulls rose into the air, screaming and flapping their wings as the *Discovery* weighed anchor and inched closer to the boat, which Motter and the wounded Prickett were rowing.

An hour later the nightmare came to an end. The unconscious Perse was taken up to the ship, and Prickett followed, the wound in his back still bleeding. Several men lowered themselves to the boat, and when they saw that Greene was dead, they unceremoniously dumped his body overboard.

Prickett later wrote the obituary of this evil, clever man in his diary, saying, "Greene made reckoning to receive great matters from these people. He received more than he looked for, and that most suddenly."

The savage whom Prickett had wounded was taken onto the *Discovery*, where he died a few hours later. His knife, several members of the shrunken company said, was similar to those used by the natives of Java. Perse did not regain consciousness, and a few day later he, too, was dead.

The survivors' situation was desperate. Only nine men, including the injured Prickett, were still alive. Provisions had dwindled almost to the vanishing point. Bylot, who took complete command now, knew it would not be possible to cross the Atlantic before obtaining fresh supplies. So, in spite of the danger of another native attack and the strong possibility that the *Discovery* might be smashed on rocks, he sailed to the northern side of Digges Island and anchored as close to the shore as he dared.

Both cannon were loaded. The injured Prickett manned one and young Syms took charge of the other. Bylot stayed with them, staring at the forest through Henry Hudson's glass, and the other six went ashore, armed with blunderbusses, pistols, and cutlasses. The savages appeared almost immediately, but a shot from Syms' cannon landed in their midst. With lucky aim it killed several natives, and the rest disappeared.

The mutineers were not plagued by them again. In the next few days a number of trips to the island were made, and hundreds of birds were bagged and thrown into barrels of salt.

Glad to leave the accursed place, the little company finally set sail. Juet advised that they go to the Newfoundland fishing banks, where civilized men would give them salt cod and bread. He was reminded that the season was too far advanced and that the fishing fleets had undoubtedly returned to their home ports across the sea. His mind unsettled, the old man insisted that it was the custom of the fishermen to leave large caches of bread, salt cod, halibut, and other food on shore for emergency use.

No one believed this fanciful tale. Prickett urged that they sail to Ireland, "where cereals grew in abundance." Everyone agreed, and Bylot insisted that each man receive only a half-bird and a handful of meal each day.

Juet, whose mind was deteriorating rapidly, began to burn the feathers of the gulls and eat the tiny bits of meat that clung to them. The others were so hungry they soon followed his example.

The last of the grain and peas was consumed. Mathues was forced to display great ingenuity, and fried the birds' bones in candle grease until they were crisp, then cut the taste of the grease with vinegar. Each man received one pound of the fried bones and a cup of vinegar. Bylot insisted that this meager fare was a week's rations.

Juet began to suffer severe hallucinations, and several times each day insisted he could see the coast of Ireland.

The men were too weak to wash dried blood from the *Discovery*'s decks or clean the blankets of those who had died. It was an ordeal to take the helm, and only Bylot was strong enough to stand on his two feet when performing this duty. The others were so exhausted they were compelled to sit on a chair they brought to the quarterdeck for the purpose.

They sailed on through choppy seas, and their torture became worse. When a line broke or a sail ripped, no one was strong enough to climb up into the rigging and make repairs. Gradually the ship deteriorated, and her sailing time became slower each day. Bylot, himself scarcely able to stagger from one end of the *Discovery* to the other, carried a strip of leather that he fashioned into a crude whip so he could beat the others into performing essential tasks.

The sails, Prickett wrote in his diary in a shaking hand, had become "brown skeletons of leaves."

Juet became raving mad one morning, talked incessantly for hours, and then suddenly dropped dead. The others nudged his body overboard.

The eight survivors became so listless that the only duty they were capable of performing was that of taking the helm for short periods. Virtually all hope was abandoned.

Then, on September 6, they sighted the shore of Ireland, but were unwilling to trust their own eyes. A short time later a Cornish fishing master hailed them, took them in tow, and sailed into the harbor of the little town of Berehaven, in Bantry Bay.

The ordeal was not yet over. The villagers were very poor, and refused to extend charity to these tattered, scrawny Englishmen. In final desperation, Bylot pawned the *Discovery*'s cable to the Cornishman, and the famished mutineers were at last able to eat their fill of bread, beef, and peas. They bought beer, too, but discovered that a few sips made them dizzy.

Finally the master of an English merchantman came to their assistance. They needed help in order to reach England, the master declared, and he would hang any local sailor who refused to assist them. The reluctant seamen relented, but charged the outrageous fee of three pounds, ten shillings each in wages to take the *Discovery* to Plymouth.

Once there, basic repairs were made. After two weeks of eating solid food again, the mutineers were strong enough to take charge of the ship, and sailed on to London without further incident.

One of the most significant—and tragic—voyages in the history of exploration came to her inglorious end.

XIII

Glory and Retribution

ह‍॰

THE *Discovery* reached London on October 20, and Bylot went at once to report to Sir Thomas Smith, taking Prickett with him. Four days later the owners, sitting as a court of inquiry, interrogated each of the survivors, and it was the unanimous opinion of these gentlemen that the mutineers should be hanged. But they made no such recommendation to the government, and not until the following year was one of the survivors, Edward Wilson, even questioned by the High Court of Admiralty.

The clever Prickett was largely responsible for this shocking miscarriage of justice. He produced Henry Hudson's charts and maps, which accurately reproduced the eastern and southern shores of Hudson Bay. The western shore did not appear, and Prickett insisted that the bay was an open sea which would lead to the Orient. Bylot said the same.

Merchants and mariners rejoiced that the northwest passage

had been found. The name of the martyred Henry Hudson was on every Englishman's lips. The mutineers, who were familiar with this previously unknown sea, were too valuable now to be hanged.

A new company was formed under the name of The Discoverers of the Northwest Passage, and King James granted it a charter. In the spring of 1612 two ships were sent to Hudson Bay, the *Resolution* and Hudson's *Discovery*. Bylot actually sailed as second mate of the *Resolution*, Edward Wilson was her surgeon, and Prickett her bo's'n's mate!

The Admiralty did not forget the mutineers, however. Bylot became a captain and master of the *Discovery* in his own right, sailing her to Hudson Bay himself on two of her many voyages there. By 1617 he—and many others—had explored the whole west coast of Hudson Bay and could find no outlet to the Pacific.

In that same year a noted explorer, William Baffin—after whom the great island north of Hudson Bay and the sea to its east are named—ended the speculation. "There is no passage nor hope of a passage to the East from Hudson Bay," he told the world.

In 1617 the Admiralty began a new investigation in earnest, and in 1618 its High Court finally tried the mutineers. Nicholas Syms was excused, having been a minor at the time, and therefore was judged not responsible. Bylot, who had now acquired a reputation as a distinguished adventurer-explorer, also escaped prosecution. How he accomplished this agile feat is unknown. Three other mutineers had died during the intervening years.

But Abacuk Prickett, Francis Clemens, Edward Wilson, and Bennett Mathues were placed on trial. The evidence against them had been obscured by time. Prickett was still a clever manipulator who could shape half-truths to suit his own ends, and the whole blame for the mutiny was placed on Greene, William Wilson, John Thomas, and Robert Juet, none of whom were alive, none of whom could point an accusing finger at their fellow conspirators.

A verdict of "Not Guilty" was rendered, and the four men were set free.

From the time of the derelict *Discovery*'s return to England in 1611, Henry Hudson was universally recognized as the greatest explorer of his day. The Dutch were sending new expeditions to the great river he had found, and the English made Hudson Bay their own.

Katherine Hudson, grieving for her husband and son, must have enjoyed the adulation, the knowledge that Henry Hudson had won immortality. But she was undoubtedly distracted by practical considerations. She was almost destitute, and her future was as precarious as her present.

This quiet, unassuming woman who had lived her whole life in shadows, suddenly became actively aggressive. She went in person to the directors of the East India Company and requested that employment be given her son, Richard. Sir Thomas Smith and his colleagues obliged at once, even providing money for Richard Hudson's sea gear.

He was sent to the Far East on a ship called the *Samaritan*, and thus began a long and distinguished career. He worked in India for a time as a trader, and subsequently was one of the first Europeans to be given a permit to dwell in Imperial Japan. There he represented the East India Company with such success that he was sent back to India as principal representative of the company in the Bay of Bengal. He prospered, his home at Balasor was almost as large as that of the local Rajah's, and eventually he amassed a considerable fortune.

On a trip to England late in the 1630's he became involved in a dispute with his superiors, who threatened to send him to prison for some reason which has never been made public but apparently was concerned with finances. He successfully defied the directors, however, and returned to Balasor, where he died in 1644. He was regarded as a man of great distinction both in India and at home.

Several of his many children migrated to the New World which their grandfather had done so much to open to settlement and commerce. The present-day descendants of Henry Hudson who live in the United States trace their lineage through Richard.

Katherine Hudson was not satisfied with finding a place for her young son, but had to think of herself, too. She called a second time on the directors of the East India Company and asked that she be given employment. She had a good head for figures, she told them, and was interested in the expanding world trade in whose cause her husband had lost his life. Few women in that time worked for a living in honorable vocations, and there were virtually none in the merchant trade. But the embarrassed Sir Thomas and his colleagues were in no position to refuse Mrs. Hudson's demand.

With great reluctance they found a place for her in their London offices, no doubt thinking of the position as a form of pension. Katherine Hudson surprised them. She proved to be a remarkably shrewd bargainer, and she quickly recognized the weaknesses and strengths of the men who traveled to the far parts of the earth on behalf of the company. Within a very few years she had made a secure position for herself in the company's ranks.

Now, having tasted financial success for the first time in her poverty-stricken life, she wanted to earn still more. Making her plans with great care, she decided to travel to India herself in order to engage in the rapidly growing indigo trade there. Mere men were no match for this determined woman, and she wrung special concessions from the company that would enable her to show a larger personal profit.

Having obtained the terms she wanted, she sailed to India, setting herself up in a house at Ahmadabad. She had a keen eye for bargains, and liked various local fabrics. Reasoning that if she thought they were attractive, other women in England would feel the same, she began to buy large quantities of cottons on her own initiative.

When the company refused to grant her the privileges on the fabrics that she had been given in the indigo trade, she wrote her employers two sharp, unyielding letters. The directors wearily submitted to her demands, and in 1622 Mrs. Hudson returned to England a wealthy woman.

She retired to the same house in which she had lived with her husband and children, and spent the last two years of her life in comfort, enjoying the fruits of her labor. She had many friends, but preferred the company of her son, Oliver, and his children, and seemed content. She was honored by everyone as the widow of the great explorer, and on at least two occasions she was received at court, a rare privilege for a woman who was a middle-aged commoner.

Mrs. Hudson died in September, 1624, leaving her estate to her two surviving sons.

In the months immediately prior to her death, she became interested in erecting a memorial to her husband in London, but the project languished after she died. No such statue was needed, however. The immigrants who went by the thousands and tens of thousands to the New World, the beaver pelts, lumber, and other natural resources of America that flowed to England in a steady, golden stream, constituted a far more enduring monument to the name and achievements of Henry Hudson.

Principal Bibliography

Asher, G. M., *Henry Hudson the Navigator*, Hakluyt Society, London, 1860.

Bacon, Edgar M., *Henry Hudson, His Times and His Voyages*, G. P. Putnam's Sons, New York, 1907.

Hakluyt, Richard, *The Principal Navigators' Voyages*, James MacLehose & Sons, Glasgow, 1903.

———, *Voyages*, Hakluyt Society, London, 1850.

Hudson, Henry, *The Adventures of Henry Hudson*, D. Appleton & Co., New York, 1842.

Janvier, Thomas A., *Henry Hudson*, Harper & Bros., New York, 1909.

Murphy, Henry, *Henry Hudson in Holland*, Martinus Nijhoff, The Hague, 1909.

Powys, Llewelyn, *Henry Hudson*, The Bodley Head, London, 1927.

Read, John M., Jr., *An Historical Inquiry Concerning Henry Hudson*, Joel Mansell, London, 1866.

Winsor, Justin, *Narrative & Critical History of America*, Houghton, Mifflin & Co., Cambridge (Mass.), 1884.